Long Stays in
AMERICA

Long Stays in AMERICA

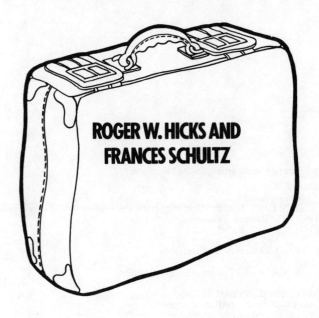

ROGER W. HICKS AND
FRANCES SCHULTZ

DAVID & CHARLES
Newton Abbot   London

HIPPOCRENE BOOKS
New York

Whilst every attempt has been made to ensure that the information contained in this book is accurate at the time of going to press, the authors and publishers can accept no responsibility for any errors or omissions.

British Library Cataloguing in Publication

Hicks, Roger W.
   Long stays in America.
   1. United States – Handbooks, manuals, etc
   I. Title   II. Schultz, Frances
   917.3′04927   E158

   ISBN 0-7153-8730-8 (Great Britain)

Typeset by Typesetters (Birmingham) Ltd
Smethwick, West Midlands
and printed in Great Britain
by A. Wheaton & Co Ltd, Hennock Road, Exeter
for David & Charles Publishers plc
Brunel House   Newton Abbot   Devon

Published in the United States of America
by Hippocrene Books Inc
171 Madison Avenue, New York, NY 10016

ISBN 0-87052-342-2 (United States)

Contents

For Arthur and Marion Schultz

Introduction:
My New-Found Land, My America

This book is intended for anyone who is taking more than a short holiday in the United States. As a rough guide, we have assumed stays of between a month or two and three or four years, although even the person who is visiting the country for a couple of weeks will find plenty that is useful, and we have also discussed the possibility of longer stays, including permanent immigration, in several places.

The longer your intended stay, the more thoroughly you need to plan and research your trip. A holiday should be just that: a release from the pressures of work, a time for relaxing and enjoying yourself. There are excellent hotels in many price ranges in America, and all sorts of restaurants, and huge areas dedicated to recreation and amusement, whether your tastes run to the majesty of the Californian High Sierra or the relentless jollity of Disneyland. But a stay of a few months, where you want to learn something about the country, is likely to throw you more upon your own resources; and if you plan on living and working in the United States, you will not only have to deal with American bureaucracy (which can be Byzantine), but also with American business methods and ethics, American housing and shops, American health insurance, and quite possibly American schools for your children.

Inevitably, a book such as this must assume that the reader has virtually no knowledge of the United States, except perhaps what everyone gleans from American television programmes and American movies. Equally inevitably, some of our readers will be familiar with the country from repeated visits, and will only be interested in those things which are relevant to actually moving to the United States. We have attempted, therefore, to make each chapter as self-contained as possible, so that you need read only what interests you.

Although inflation makes actual prices meaningless – they date too fast – and the fluctuations in the exchange rate simply compound the problem, we have referred throughout the book to a 'rule of two', which holds generally good, that if you *halve* prices in dollars, or *double* figures in pounds sterling, you get a good general idea of relative values. For example, if you are asked to pay $4 for something in the US, it is more or less the equivalent of a price of £2 in Britain. Where individual prices vary markedly from this average, we have said so. It is a crude rule of thumb, but it is accurate enough for a general guide, so long as the exchange rate remains in the $1.10–$1.80 range.

Finally, we must confess to a bias. The United States of America is a huge country, and it is impossible to write about it as a whole. The old East, the old South, the Midwest and the West are all very different from one another, and those broad divisions are only a beginning; the individual states each have their own laws, geography and personalities. Even within a state, there can be surprising variation: the mellow, almost seasonless climate of Southern California is very different from the blasting heat of central California or the more European north of the state, where snow falls in the winter, and the cultural variations of the three areas are no less than the climatic ones. Although by birth we come one from the Old World and one from upstate New York, we are by temperament Westerners. Our favourite states are west of the Rockies: Nevada, Utah, New Mexico, California. If our preferences sometimes seem too clear, we can at best make only half-hearted apologies, because one of the most wonderful things about the United States is that you can hunt for and find a place that suits you. We hope that this book will make it easier for you to do just that.

1

The Land of the Free

Almost everything that you have ever heard about the United States of America – good and bad – is true. It is a nation so vast that it can contain everything, including paradoxes and flat contradictions. In California, you do not need a licence to carry a .44 Magnum revolver strapped to your hip (unless you wear a coat and conceal the fact that you are carrying a gun), but you can get a $25 ticket for jaywalking if you do not walk to the end of the street and cross at the traffic lights. In parts of Nevada, prostitution, bars and gambling are major industries; in parts of Kansas, by contrast, you need to be a member of a private club just in order to get a drink with a meal. The bars in many states have no fixed hours – they close in the small hours of the morning – but it is usually illegal to drink a can of beer in the street, and an offence to have an open bottle of liquor (or even an empty beer can) in the passenger compartment of a car.

In a country which covers more than 3½ million square miles, and which is home to nearly 250 million people, such variations are not just understandable; they are perhaps inevitable. But in order to make sense of them, it becomes obvious that you have to break the country down into smaller units. States would be the obvious choice, except that there are fifty of them, and that it is comparatively easy to group them together for the purposes of generalisations. There are several ways of doing this, but the two most usual are the 'Three Countries' model, and the 'Sunbelt' model.

The Three Countries model is based on the historical development of the United States. The Eastern Seaboard is the first 'country', a nation settled in the seventeenth and eighteenth centuries by a comparatively few emigrants, mostly British but with a few Dutch and Germans. They established first an agricultural society and then, in the north, an industrial one; the two came into conflict in the American Civil War, and were uneasily reunited. Meanwhile, the second 'country' was being created in the early-to-mid nineteenth century: the huge agricultural areas of the Midwest were being opened up. The Midwesterners sent their sons to fight on the Union side, simply to preserve the Union; but they did not generally have strong feelings about it and it would probably not have mattered very much to them if the Confederacy had won. Finally, in the latter part of the nineteenth century, the far West became the third 'country' — a process which continues even into the twentieth century.

This is, of course, a massive oversimplification. It takes no account of French America, which was mostly in Louisiana, and very little of Spanish America, which included Florida, Texas and California. The former was dealt with by purchase — the United States simply bought Louisiana from France in 1803 — and the latter by 'manifest destiny', which was the American version of *Lebensraum*, or simple territorial aggression. California, for example, had been settled by the Spanish in the eighteenth century: the *pueblo* (village) of Our Lady the Queen of the Angels, now known as the City of Los Angeles, was founded in 1781. The Three Countries model also neglects Hawaii, which voluntarily (and somewhat curiously, in view of its geographical isolation) joined the Union in 1959, and Alaska, the 'Last Frontier', which was bought as a territory from Russia in 1867 but which remained comparatively unsettled until well into the present century, and only became a state in 1959 after mineral exploitation had begun to assume really major importance.

Nevertheless, this model does explain a good deal about the cultural variations of the United States. In the East, the New England states of Connecticut, Maine, Massachusetts, New Hampshire, Rhode Island and Vermont were originally settled mostly by religious enthusiasts of one sort or another, and rural Pennsylvania is much the same. Obsessed with the World, the Flesh and the Devil, the Puritans were particularly worried about sex and alcohol, and they bequeathed legal codes which reflect this. To this day, long lists of prohibitions, particularly in public places, are to be found all over the Puritan East; in Pennsylvania roadside rest stops, for example, there are signs which not only forbid the consumption of alcohol, but also 'lewd and lascivious conduct, including but not limited to sexual intercourse and soliciting for the purposes of prostitution'. One

10

cannot help wondering what sort of person (other than Puritans) would go to motorway service stations for their kicks . . .

The New England states are also the most formal and stuffy. Men wear business suits and short hair, and women do not as a rule wear trousers, at least to work. In the evening, people dress up to go out; a man dressed in typical Californian style, with training shoes, open-necked shirt and casual trousers, would raise eyebrows in many restaurants and would be refused service in the more expensive ones — something which would only happen in the most expensive (or pretentious) places in his home state.

This Puritan influence also percolates into the neighbouring states to a certain extent — Ohio is about as far west as it reaches — but as you go south and west it softens considerably. Delaware and Maryland are much less obviously restrictive and formal than New England proper; New York State (which extends to the Canadian border, over 400 miles from New York City) is not too bad, and the Virginias, the Carolinas and Georgia show nothing like the Puritanism of the North. Of all the Eastern states, Florida is the odd one out; its Spanish antecedents make it quite different from its Eastern neighbours, and more like the West, though Eastern organised crime likes to vacation there.

Alabama, Illinois, Indiana, Kentucky, Michigan, Mississippi, Tennessee and Wisconsin are reckoned by some to be a part of the Midwest, and by others to be Eastern states. A good Westerner will contend that the East begins at the Mississippi river (or at the Rockies if he or she is a *real* Westerner), but to an Easterner these states represent the beginnings of the Midwest. Then again, some will call the Dakotas, Kansas, Montana, Nebraska, Oklahoma and Wyoming the West, reserving the term Midwest for Arkansas, Illinois, Indiana, Iowa, Michigan, Minnesota, Mississippi, Missouri and Wisconsin; what we call the West then becomes the Far West. In fact, the states listed at the very beginning of this paragraph are transitional: they are agricultural, but they tend to support smaller, poorer farms than the vast and rich Kansas and Oklahoma plains, and traditionally there was more variety, with horse-ranching and cotton and tobacco farming, in place of the endless wheat-fields of the plains states. Nowadays, the wheat-fields no longer stretch from horizon to horizon in Kansas: over-

11

production, rather than underproduction, was the problem.

Culturally, too, these semi Midwest states are less easily pigeonholed. There is a strong division, along Civil War lines, between North and South, and the 'poor white' and the black inhabitants often live in serious poverty, particularly in Kentucky and Tennessee; the more fortunate of them work on reasonably prosperous farms. Alabama and Mississippi are also productive agricultural states. In the north, Wisconsin's title of 'America's Dairyland' (it actually appears on car licence plates) is no idle boast, while Illinois and Michigan are famous for industry, with a good deal of agriculture in between the cities. As a rule, the further south you go, the more important religious fundamentalism becomes: this is where you begin to meet significant numbers of people who believe in the literal truth of every word of the Bible, though it must be said that there is a fair sprinkling of these all over the country.

The heart of the Midwest (at least by our definition) is made up of Iowa, Kansas, Missouri, Nebraska and Oklahoma, with the Dakotas, Minnesota and Montana arguably a part of the same terrain. The first five states listed are archetypal 'big sky' country, with vast open prairies supporting wheat, maize, cattle and hogs; the others offer more variety in both geography and economy, but are still primarily agricultural. These are the states least visited by tourists, or indeed anyone else: like any farm, they go on working day in, day out, without any major events to disturb the tenor of the years and the decades. There is far more to see in the northern and western Midwest states than you might imagine, but it cannot be denied that Kansas and Oklahoma are not particularly exciting, and that the people are inclined to be stolid, old-fashioned and somewhat repressive. They cling to their religion, without being fanatical, and they are helpful and friendly; but they expect you to do things their way, and if you try to persuade them that there are other ways they rapidly become stubborn, then downright hostile.

From a geographical point of view, Arkansas and Louisiana might be placed in the Midwest, but their ties are more with the old South. Their agriculture has more in common with Mississippi and Alabama, and like those states, there is also considerable poverty in many areas, something that is quite rare in the rest of the Midwest.

12

Likewise, Texas is undeniably in the same longitude as the Midwest, but its vast size means that while the northern and eastern parts fit the Midwestern pattern fairly well, its south and west are much more a part of the far West, which is how it is considered here. On the other hand, although Texas is more affluent than most of the old South, largely because of oil, there is also no doubt where its political sympathies lie; like those of the old South, they are well to the right.

Moving over to the far West, we have Arizona, California, Colorado, Idaho, New Mexico, Nevada, Oregon, Utah, Washington and Wyoming – all the states west of, or straddling, the Rockies – plus Texas. Out here, distances are vast and much of the land in the south is either marginal or just plain desert. The state of Nevada is so huge, and so deserted, that the US Government tests atom bombs in parts of the desert without disturbing anyone much, though the more devoted Westerner will ask why they can't do it in, say, Pennsylvania and rid the world of a few eyesores at the same time; or better still, in Washington DC and get rid of the interfering bureaucrats who keep sticking their noses into state affairs.

In the north, in Washington, Oregon, Idaho, and northern and coastal California, there is a good deal of farming and agriculture. The same is true on the eastern side of those states which straddle the Rockies, especially Wyoming and Colorado. But Arizona, Utah, Nevada, much of New Mexico, and inland California are mostly desert, and often staggeringly beautiful desert. The Grand Canyon in Arizona is merely the biggest and best-known of the desert landscapes sculpted by wind and water which are found throughout these states; in Zion Canyon in Utah, for example, there is a canyon with walls between 1,000ft and 2,000ft (300–600m) high – but less than 20ft (6m) apart at the canyon's narrowest point. In California's Yosemite, great walls and domes of glacier-polished granite adorn the High Sierra.

By contrast with the states to the east, these Western states like to do things their own way. The federal 55mph limit (still in force at the time of writing, though under increasing attack) is simply not taken seriously; in Nevada, anything between 55mph and 70mph brings merely a slap on the wrist in the form of a $5 'energy conservation' ticket; you have to exceed 70mph to get a speeding ticket. In California, it is quite usual to be tooling along at 60–65mph and to be passed by a California Highway Patrol officer who pays no attention at all. Again, with the possible exceptions of Arizona and Texas, the far West is the least oppressively religious part of the United States. There are still plenty of churches, and they are well patronised, but there is not generally the relentless determination to impose their views on unbelievers which is sometimes found further East.

It will have become obvious by now that there has been curiously little mention of cities and of industry in the Three Countries model. This is partly because American cities are not always typical of the states in which they are located, and partly because the Sunbelt model is more use when considering cities and industry.

The first part of that statement might seem a little strange – after all, is Omaha not typical of Nebraska, and is Boston not typical of Massachusetts? – but it is still readily defensible. With few exceptions, the major cities of the United States are vastly more cosmopolitan than their surroundings: St Louis, Missouri, and Minneapolis/St Paul, Minnesota, are attractive cities by any standards, and someone who would find the rural areas of those states unbearably oppressive could readily live in either city. By contrast, someone who could not stand the abrasive brashness of New York City might well find that a smaller city such as Rochester, way upstate, was considerably more congenial. It is also true that the big cities tend to be very much more regulated than the surrounding states: the left-wing government of San Francisco, for example, would find itself at home in any large socialist-run city in the United Kingdom, with its massive grants to fringe causes and, for example, a city ordnance requiring that 1 per cent of all building costs be spent on art. When you consider that a major development could easily cost a hundred million dollars, you wonder where they are going to find a million dollars' worth of art to decorate it . . .

Much more important, though, is the role of the Sunbelt model, which traces the shift of wealth and production away from agriculture and the heavy industry of the north-east towards the high-technology industries which are increasingly located in the South and West. 'Silicon Valley' in California is well known, but many electronics and computer-programming companies are based elsewhere in California and in Arizona; aircraft and aerospace companies are definitely stronger west of Denver; and all other kinds of manufacturing where the value of the product lies more in the ingenuity of the process than in the cost of the materials are typical of the Sunbelt, which includes mostly the south-west but also embraces Florida, a part of the world which some see as America's next California, in the sense of experiencing an exponential growth of population. Proponents of the Sunbelt theory are fixated with the sun: they also refer to 'sunrise' industries (high-technology, where a developed nation such as the United States or the United Kingdom can apply the benefits of mass education and a tradition of technical experience) and 'sunset' industries such as steel smelting and even car manufacture, where countries which can draw on low labour costs have the advantage.

The attractions of the Sunbelt are obvious. Most people like warm sunny weather, and there is plenty of that in the Sunbelt. Irrigation takes care of the desert, at least in the immediate vicinity of the home, and air-conditioning takes the sting out of too-hot weather in a way that heating in too-cold weather cannot hope to match. The creative people, so the argument goes, have had the sense to move; they have left the old cities of the north-east to decay. Certainly, New York City, Pittsburgh, Philadelphia, Detroit, Cleveland and the like do tend to look very weary and battered when compared with the bright new areas of Phoenix, Tucson and Dallas/Fort Worth; but is at least arguable that with cities, as with people, age brings its problems. The *barrios* of Los Angeles are not exactly model villages, though it is certainly true that most of downtown Los Angeles is a good deal cleaner and more impressive than most of downtown New York, and LA's Watts is certainly no worse than the Big Apple's Harlem.

With either model, Alaska and Hawaii are the odd men out, and that is generally the way that they are going to stay throughout the book. Hawaii is of course a tropical island, whose main industries are tourism, agriculture and military bases; with the exception of Hawaii itself and Oahu, which is heavily Americanised, the outlying islands and indeed many areas of the main islands are fairly pastoral and primitive. Communications really preclude Hawaii's being included in the Sunbelt, and it remains a special case. Other than as a holiday resort, or in connection with the military, it is hard to imagine that many Britons will go there.

Alaska is at the other extreme of climate from Hawaii. It is truly the 'Frozen North', with a good part of the state lying inside the Arctic Circle. Often called the 'Last Frontier', it is still a place where the old Frontier virtues and vices go hand in hand: self sufficiency, a degree of lawlessness and a good deal of serious drinking. The extremely harsh climate means that most amusements are sought indoors, with only the very hardy venturing out; the main reasons why people go anywhere outside Anchorage are for mineral exploration (including working on oil rigs) and mining, though the old industry of fishing should not be discounted. The possibilities of earning a lot of money in return for hard and sometimes dangerous work exist in Alaska, and it is reputed to be one of the easier places to get work illegally: the frontier tradition of not asking too many questions of a man who is prepared to work hard is still a reality in many places. Even so, Alaska is sufficiently remote, and unusual as a destination for visitors, to be not really within the compass of a guide such as this.

The question of climate is of course a major factor to consider when choosing somewhere to live or visit in the United States. From tropical to arctic, there is something for everyone, and within the generalisations which can be made about each state there are all sorts of surprises. For example, who but a geographer who had studied the area would expect snow around the Grand Canyon? Countless pictures have conditioned us to accept it as desert, and in the popular mind deserts are hot, at least during the daytime. Still more surprising, who would imagine that it could be raining on the rim of the canyon, but that the rain would evaporate before it reached the canyon floor?

The brief descriptions of regional climate in Appendix 1 may give some idea of the climate in each state, but what they cannot readily do is to convey the meaning of extremes of climate which are outside the experience of the average Briton. For example, at about 15°F (−9°C), a man's breath will freeze on his moustache − something which few Britons will ever have experienced − and in upstate New York, temperatures of 0°F (−18°C) are common in winter. In Alaska and much of Canada, −40°F (which is also −40°C) is by no means unusual, and all sorts of strange things happen at these temperatures: exposed flesh freezes on to bare

16

metal, plastics which are flexible at room temperature become rigid and crack like glass, and most batteries, other than lead-acid car batteries, cease to deliver any power. If your car breaks down, and you are not rescued by a passing motorist in a few hours or if you cannot walk to shelter, you will die.

At the other extreme, desert temperatures mean that you lose water at a remarkable rate: a gallon of water *per person per day* is generally regarded as a realistic quantity. Every year, ill-prepared motorists venture too far off the road in Death Valley, break down, and die of thirst.

Snow can fall in quantities which are beyond the conception of the average Briton. In a country where 15 *inches* would be a heavy snowfall, it is hard to imagine what 15 *yards* (540 inches) of snow might be like – but that is what falls in parts of Sequoia National Park in central California in a year. High passes may be closed for months by snow: the Tioga pass at the north-east of Yosemite National Park is frequently closed from September to May. In Rocky Mountain National Park, the highest road is over 12,500ft (4,580m) high; even in August, snow lingers on the ground and the wind is piercingly cold.

Flash floods are something else which desert dwellers are aware of, but which catch the unwary every year. Desert rainstorms are sudden and heavy, and the *arroyos* (dry river beds) can fill up in minutes with a torrent powerful enough to sweep away a motor car, never mind a person.

It is of course possible to overestimate the importance of climate: with the right clothes, and air-conditioning or central heating as appropriate, you can handle a considerably greater range of temperatures than you may be used to. It is also important to realise that for the most part, British houses are appallingly ill-designed to withstand even the modest extremes of our own climate. In winter, the insulation is pitifully inadequate (double glazing has been the norm for many years in most of the states which suffer from harsh winters) and in the summer it is virtually impossible to get adequate shade and a natural circulation of cool air; in the United States, domestic air-conditioners are regarded as essential to civilised living in warm climates. You may find however that Americans overreact to their own climate, overheating to the point of stuffiness in winter and overcooling to the point of discomfort in the summer.

LSA-B

Taking all of this into consideration, you should make allowance for the fact that in most of the United States the extremes of temperature are considerably greater than they are in the British Isles. If you are the sort of person who wilts when the temperature climbs above 85°F (30°C), then you are likely to find most of the country too warm in the summer, with the exception of some of the cities in the mountains: New York in August, with temperatures in the 90s Fahrenheit (30s Centigrade) and very high humidity, is particularly uncomfortable. If you like invigorating walks on brisk winter's days, stay away from Southern California — though you can always drive into the Sierra Madre mountains, where the combination of sun and snow is delightful. If you can't stand cold, then steer clear of most of the north of the country, and check those abstracts of temperatures and rainfall carefully: in Georgia, which most people imagine is warm all the year round, because that is the way it always appears in movies, the winters can be cruel.

2

America the Beautiful

Even those who have lived in America all their lives, and who have done their best to see as much of the country as possible, will freely admit that it is impossible to see all that there is to see in a single lifetime. Much of the country is very beautiful indeed, and often the scenery is unique: the Painted Desert and the Grand Canyon in Arizona, and Bryce and Zion National Parks in Utah, are sights the like of which are probably not to be found anywhere else on the planet – certainly not anywhere that is anything like accessible. Even where the scenery is not unique in kind, it is often on a scale and of such loveliness that it has no equal: this can be said of much of California's Pacific Coast Highway. On top of all that, there are man-made attractions such as Disneyland and its imitators, huge amusement parks which have no real equal in Europe.

America's tourist attractions alone are enough to warrant a journey, but for anyone who is considering moving to the United States there is a much more pressing reason to go on an extended vacation and to see as much of the country as possible. It is extremely unlikely that you will dislike the whole country so much that you will feel unable to live there, but it is possible; and it is more than likely that there will be some places with which you will feel an instantaneous rapport, and others to which you will take an equally instantaneous dislike.

Of course, if you already have the offer or at least the possibility of a job in a particular area, the obvious thing to do is to concentrate on that area. As well as checking out the city itself, you will also want to know where the local recreation spots are, how to reach them, and so forth. You may also want to check out feasible commuting distances; a friend of the authors works in New York City, but commutes every day from his farm 50 miles out of the city. Throughout the summer – basically, when there is not snow on the ground –

he rides a motorcycle; the rest of the time, he uses a car. He says that if he had to use a car all year round, he would not be able to stand the daily journey.

If you do have a particular location in mind, you will also need to check out housing costs, and to see what you get for your money; the degree of automation in American houses is very high, and many household appliances such as stoves, washing machines, dishwashers and air-conditioners may be regarded as fixtures and fittings – or they may not, and this can make a difference of two or three thousand dollars, or even more, when it comes to setting up house. By the same token, if you have children it is as well to take a look at the school system, and to see whether you want to use the local public (ie state) schools, which are free, or to pay for a private school – or to send the children to boarding school in the UK. You can see what the local standard of living is like, and check out the cost of living against your prospective salary, as well as checking your salary against the going rate in the area (more about this in Chapter 11).

You will have to bear in mind that American vacations are usually very short (Chapter 11 again), and if you are working under American conditions of employment you are unlikely to be able to get away as often, or for as long, as you would like, so while (for example) you could easily drive from Los Angeles to Yosemite, you would have to fly in order to get there from anywhere east of the Rockies; equally, if you adore New York City and you have the chance of a posting to Dallas, do not imagine that you will get to the Big Apple all that often. Even within a state, distances can be much greater than you think: Rochester, New York, where Eastman Kodak is located, is about four hundred miles from New York City, and San Francisco is about the same distance north of Los Angeles.

In the light of all this, it would be extremely rash to go to the United States for the first time *after* you have arranged a job, accommodation, perhaps schools for the children, and so forth. Ideally, you should spend at least a month getting the feel of the country, though expense may well rule this out; at the very least, you should spend a couple of weeks there, *with your spouse and children if applicable* (see Chapter 5), taking a week at the proposed job location and a week travelling further afield. An exception to this general rule might be in the case of contract work (see Chapter 3).

The technicalities and logistics of getting there are covered in Chapter 7, and Chapter 12, which deals with relaxation, has more to say about vacationing inside America, but for a first-time visitor or tourist the first thing to learn is that it is virtually impossible to survive without your own transport. New York is a notable exception, with a reasonably cheap and efficient (but filthy and sometimes dangerous) underground railway system, and if you stay in the very centre of many other cities you will be able to get about; in San Francisco, you can even walk, and the Bay Area Rapid Transit System (BART) also serves some of the suburbs. But if you want to see the country, or even if you want to check out housing in the suburbs, you will have to have a car. This gives you two options. Either you can drive everywhere, or you can travel to the area by air, rail or bus, and then hire cars at each location.

If time and money permit it, the former is the ideal approach. It gives you a chance to appreciate the scale of the country, to see as much of it as possible, and to meet as many American people as possible, which is one of the fascinations of the country. Car rental is reasonably cheap in the United States, though it pays to shop around, and it is important to note that the advertised prices rarely include collision damage waiver (CDW) or passenger accident insurance (PAI). Unless you pay extra for CDW, you are liable for any collision damage to the car, though there is usually a maximum of around $2,500 or so. It is, therefore, very foolish not to take out the extra insurance, even though it can add as much as 25–30 per cent to your daily rate. PAI is a more modest surcharge, and covers you and your passengers for medical costs as well as the usual derisory rates for loss of eyes, arms, legs and life. If you have taken out holiday insurance in the UK, there is usually little to be gained by taking out PAI as well – but read both policies carefully, just to be on the safe side.

As an aside on holiday insurance, it is worth noting that it is rarely available in the US, but that most British packages offer very good cover at surprisingly low rates. Shop around, and read the exclusions carefully: some policies offer a very much better deal on valuables than others, with a maximum per-item value for things like jewellery and cameras that is twice as high as some other policies. Note however that some holiday or business insurance packages will not insure

21

valuables unless you already have 'all risks' household insurance which covers them in the UK, and that most UK household 'all risks' insurance also covers you for up to 60 days per year world-wide. If you plan on motorcycling at all, check the insurer's attitude to that too: some classify it as a normal activity, some apply a surcharge, the same as for skiing, and some refuse to cover it at all.

Returning to car hire, you will find that some companies offer special deals which must be bought before you leave the UK, some offer special deals which are available only to British or overseas passport holders (but may still be bought in the United States), and others have promotional offers which are open to everyone. If you want to hire one-way (of which more later), the one-way drop-off charges can vary enormously, by a factor of about five to one!

Two unusual types of driving which you may wish to consider are 'motor-homes' and 'delivery driving'. American motor-homes are huge motor caravans, often capable of sleeping as many as six people (though two adults and two children are a more realistic proposition, even in thirty-footers), and equipped with every convenience, including a shower, lavatory, mains-voltage generator and refrigerator, as well as the more obvious fitments. They typically deliver only about 10 miles to the (American) gallon, but for a few dollars a night you can 'hook up' in an RV (Recreational Vehicle) park with fresh water, foul-water dump-tanks, and mains power. RVs are typically hired by the week, with an additional per-mileage charge, and one-way rentals are rarely available.

Delivery driving is a curious institution in which (almost) everyone benefits. Because of the sheer size of the United States, people sometimes need to fly back somewhere and leave their car behind, or to fly somewhere and have their car delivered there. There are several companies which exist to link up the owners of such cars with people who are looking for a cheap way to travel: they charge the vehicle owner a surprisingly modest fee, and provide insurance and a screening service for drivers. They take plenty of precautions: drivers are photographed and fingerprinted, and have to deposit a modest bond (typically $100–$200 in the mid-1980s) which is returned when they deliver the car. They must stick to an agreed route, though an allowance of about 15 per cent of the total distance is added to allow for deviations, looking for restaurants and motels, and so forth. The driver must cover about 350–400 miles per day to meet the time schedule. It is certainly a cheap way of travelling, but there are many restrictions (including a totally unrealistic clause in the contract which you sign, agreeing that you will not exceed any speed limits) and it is really only to be recommended if you are on a tight budget and travelling with at least one other person. Otherwise, motel and food bills rapidly add up to the cost of an airline ticket.

If you want to try flying and driving or a combination of Amtrak (America's passenger train network) and driving, you can save a great deal of time and road mileage, at the expense of being locked into the airline's or Amtrak's schedule. It is also worth remembering that weekly car-rental rates are usually much cheaper per day than daily rates, and that monthly rates are sometimes cheaper still. Furthermore, the more people there are in your party, the more attractive the car becomes, because unlike rail and air, the price does not increase with the number of people in the party. On the other hand, hours spent rolling through Kansas (or New England for that matter) can be tedious.

It is usually cheapest to book your additional flights at the same time that you buy your tickets to the United States, because it will usually be possible for the various flights to be consolidated onto a single ticket, with a number of flight vouchers, which brings advantages on the mileage rate: as a rule, the per-mile cost of flying decreases with increasing distance. If consolidation is not possible, another possibility is 'multi-sector' tickets; particularly in the winter months, these may be the subject of special offers from the various transatlantic carriers, and although winter may not seem to be the obvious time for a vacation, it can be a lot cheaper to travel then as well as decreasing the seduction effect of warm weather. If a place looks good in winter, the chances are that it will look even better in the summer!

One fly/drive possibility is to buy an 'open jaw' ticket, flying into, say, Boston, and flying out from, say, Los Angeles. That way, you can drive right across the country and see a great deal, without having to drive all the way back again. It is possible to drive across the country in as little as five or six days, though you will have little time for sightseeing, but eight days is a relaxed journey and fourteen days gives you plenty of time off. In the example given, the distance between

Boston and Los Angeles is about 3,000 miles, but 4,000 or even 5,000 would not be too much to allow for a more relaxed cross-country journey, with side-trips.

If you decide to use Amtrak, ask about their various special offers, and about discounts for two adults travelling together and discounts for children. Their discounting structure is complex, but there is rarely any need to pay full price for more than one member of a party. Amtrak trains are extremely slow, and not much cheaper than flying if you are on your own or if you need a sleeper on the train, but at least they do give you a chance to see some of the country, and to feel that you have *travelled*, instead of just having arrived somewhere. Ploughing across the desert gives much more of a feeling for the country than just shuttling from one airport to another. You may also wish to consider a pass giving unlimited rail travel within one or more defined zones for a given length of time.

Buses are really only recommended for the young and hardy – or at least the hardy. They are cheap and, as with Amtrak, passes are available, but bus stations are usually in the roughest part of town, and you are unlikely either to find a car-rental company there or to want to sleep in that part of town. Nevertheless, there is a certain romance to them. Greyhound is of course the best-known line; Continental Trailways is their main rival; and Green Turtle buses are very cheap old bangers, notoriously slow, though they always get there eventually, often after a breakdown or two.

However you travel, it is a good idea to try to absorb as much of the local flavour as possible. Once again, the motor car is extremely effective for this, because you see the local countryside, stop at local diners for breakfast, lunch and dinner, and overhear snatches of local conversation; you are also likely to get into conversations with people you meet along the way. The TV set in your motel room will pick up local programmes; six o'clock 'diary' local-news programmes are often a good guide to an area. You can buy a local newspaper, and listen to the local radio stations: there are literally hundreds or perhaps thousands of radio stations to choose from, and while you may only be able to pick up one or two in remote desert areas, you can take your pick of thirty or forty in, say, Los Angeles. Local newspapers probably give the best impression of neighbourhood preoccupations, and of course these are as readily available at an airport or railway station as at the roadside. Comparing the *Denver Post* with the *Visalia Times-Delta*, for example, leaves you in no doubt that Denver is a major city with serious financial institutions, still retaining a good deal of Western informality, but a trifle self-important, while the area around Visalia is farming country where nothing much happens, and news from Los Angeles and San Francisco competes with lower-key local news.

Chapter 12 has more to say about America's attractions, but three points are worth making here. The first is that you should not, and indeed cannot, attempt to embrace America indiscriminately. This applies both when you are planning your route and while you are travelling. If you are by nature a lover of cities, bias your trip towards time spent in cities; if you prefer the countryside, buy a Golden Eagle passport, which for a ridiculously low fee ($10 in 1985) entitles you to visit any and all of America's National Parks for a year. Equally, be prepared for the fact that Disneyland may strike you as tacky, or the Niagara Falls as less impressive than they have been painted. Go with your preconceptions – but remain open to having them changed.

The second point is that it is a mistake to try to see too much. It would be possible to zigzag across the country for three weeks, taking in San Francisco and the Gold Country and Yosemite and Los Angeles (with Disneyland) and the Grand Canyon and Bryce and Zion and Salt Lake City and Yellowstone National Park and Mount Rushmore and . . . but just with the recitation, the mind goes dizzy, and trying to see everything on one trip is as silly as the American tourist who announces that he is going to 'do Europe' (usually pronounced 'Yurrup') in three weeks.

Finally, it will be much more difficult on your first trip to assess both time and money requirements than it will be on subsequent visits. As a rough guide, 400 miles is a good day's drive (but perfectly feasible: the authors have frequently exceeded 500), though you must make allowance for mountain roads, which can slow you down dramatically. Do not plan to spend your entire time on the road: five or six days at a stretch is usually plenty, after which two nights in the same place are very welcome. As for money, your main concerns will be accommodation, food and gas (petrol): the car rental price can easily be established beforehand.

American motels range from the remarkably cheap to the

reasonable; hotels, especially in cities, tend to be more expensive. The Motel 6 chain, originally named for their $6 per night single fee, is a particular bargain; the cost has risen steadily until in the mid-1980s it was $17.95 single, $21.95 double, with toilet and shower – but a double room has two double beds, and the management will not blink if four people share it (preferably two parents and two children!). Motel 6 hotels are so popular, though, that in the summer season it is necessary to book well ahead: outside the vacation season, booking ahead by a single night is usually enough, and if you have stayed in a Motel 6 the previous night, they will book ahead for you for a small fee. More expensive chains, such as Best Western, will charge twice as much as a Motel 6, but the rooms are rather less spartan, there is no extra charge for television, and so forth. City-centre hotels can be three or four times as expensive as a Motel 6. Certainly, accommodation is almost invariably cheaper than in a British establishment of similar quality, but breakfast is almost never included: only the most expensive hotels are likely to offer it. Beware of 'bed and breakfast' in the United States: B & B is likely to prove more expensive than a hotel, because most B & B establishments are well-furnished and style-conscious little places designed to appeal to Yuppies (Young Upwardly Mobile Professionals, who typically drive BMWs and generally have more free money than free time to spend it in). There *are* apparently 'real' B & B places, in private homes, but they are not easy to find.

Because breakfast is not included, many diners and cheaper restaurants serve it, and it can be the economical meal of the day, particularly as most people won't want to drink with breakfast, though in some states it is possible to do so. An American habit that the visitor may find unpalatable is to serve a fried breakfast, plus eggs, on the same plate as a 'short stack' of pancakes, so that the syrup which is provided for the pancakes runs over the bacon and sausages. If this worries you, always ask if the pancakes (or waffles) are served separately. Typically, a good breakfast for two people will run at about half the price of a Motel 6 room.

How much you spend on lunch will depend on your appetites, but, for example, a pizza big enough for two and a jug of beer should cost about 50 per cent more than breakfast; at dinner, with wine, you can reckon to spend two to three times as much as at breakfast. There is more information on American eating habits in Chapter 12.

Petrol ('gas') prices have always been significantly cheaper than in the UK, typically around half as expensive. The American gallon is only four-fifths of the size of a British gallon, but it costs less than half as much, depending on the exchange rate. Obviously, therefore, mileage-per-gallon figures are lower, but the days of the 8–10mpg 'gas guzzler' are gone: nowadays, even a good-sized American car is likely to return better than 20 miles to the (American) gallon on a run, and most companies hire out Japanese imports which return mileages well into the twenties.

Even if your only purpose is a long vacation, or a getting-away-from-it-all, the United States of America is a fascinating place to visit, and not as expensive as you might think. But as already mentioned, to decide to live in the country for an extended period without visiting it first is extremely unwise, unless perhaps you are posted there by an employer (such as the Foreign Office or the armed forces) who leaves you little choice.

3
Commuting
and Contract Work

For a few people, it may be possible to live and work on both sides of the Atlantic. This sort of lifestyle is associated mainly with pop stars, movie stars, and script writers, but it is possible to do it on a very much more modest scale than this, and in many other businesses. In particular, journalists may find it attractive, and it has its merits in certain types of import/export business, such as antiques.

It is also possible to find all kinds of contract work in the United States, especially in engineering and electronics, for periods which range from a few months to several years; this possibility is explored at the end of this chapter, as the shorter contracts are in many ways intermediate between commuting and a long-term stay.

With any sort of commuting or contract work, the main things to consider are the cost of maintaining two bases; the cost of air fares; the sheer time which travelling takes; and visa availability, tax liability and liability to other government imposts such as military service (at the time of writing, mercifully in abeyance in both the UK and the US).

Costs and Time
The costs of travelling to and fro across the Atlantic, and of maintaining two bases, will depend on three things: where you base yourself; the kind of bases you choose to maintain, and the frequency with which you cross the ocean. These factors are also interwoven with the amount of time you will have to spend travelling, in a subtler way than is immediately obvious.

Unless you base yourself near a major airport with direct flights between the UK and the US, you are going to end up spending very much more on fares than the cost of the basic transatlantic flight. This is covered at greater length in

Chapter 7, but it is worth emphasising that if you decided to base yourself in, say, Birmingham, England, and Dover, Delaware, you would need to get from Birmingham to Heathrow or Gatwick at one end and from New York, Philadelphia or Baltimore to Dover at the other end – and the trains do not even run to Dover. The additional travelling expenses could easily add 25 per cent to your air fare between Britain and the US, as well as anything up to ten or twelve hours of extra travelling time. On the other hand, you can find very much cheaper accommodation a few hours out of London and out of New York City, than inside the metropolises. An additional point to consider is whether you can actually work when you are travelling: a portable computer may seem like a wonderful idea, but you can only actually use it for a fraction of the time that you spend travelling.

The kind of places you choose to live in, as well as their location, can also have an enormous influence on your costs. The cheapest approach is to stay with friends or relations on one side of the Atlantic, maintaining your paid-for base on the other. The trouble with this is that you cannot usually stay for very long, unless you come to some sort of business arrangement about paying for your accommodation, though this is perfectly feasible. Economy is not the only attraction of this system: others are security (an unoccupied home is a prime target for burglars) and freedom from property taxes of various sorts, which have to be paid whether a place is occupied or not.

Moving on to independent accommodation, you have three options. The first possibility is to maintain a pied-à-terre in one place and a proper home in the other – or, if you can live that way, a pied-à-terre in both places. You can either rent or buy a 'studio apartment' (or other euphemism for 'self-contained bed-sitting room'), but your taxation position may be easier if you rent; in the UK, you can normally only recover tax on interest paid on a loan incurred for the purpose of buying your principal residence, whereas the tax man may look more favourably on rented accommodation as a necessary business expense. We have assumed that you will prefer to base yourself for tax purposes in the UK, because, believe it or not, the Inland Revenue is inclined to be easier to deal with than the American Internal Revenue Service (IRS) which has draconian powers and does not hesitate to use them if it feels that you are trying to pull a fast one.

The second possibility is to maintain a rather grander style of accommodation in both places, which again may be either bought or rented; in this case, buying, with its attendant capital appreciation, may be a better idea, though you will need a good accountant if you are to receive much allowance against tax. If you do decide to buy, it is well worth considering a mobile-home or trailer (in English, an over-sized caravan), for your American base, as described in Chapter 8.

Thirdly, you can maintain a permanent establishment in one country, and live in short-term rented or hotel accommo-dation in the other. Short-term rents are rarely practical, for two reasons. First, unless you plan on spending long periods in a place, they are expensive and more trouble to find than they are worth, and secondly, you have the difficulty and expense of setting up house each time you move. Hotels are, for most people, suitable only for short-term accommoda-tion, but it may be that if you only need to spend a few weeks at a time in a place they can be the cheapest option – if you are only used to paying daily rates, it may surprise you how much lower weekly rates can be, and some hotels such as the celebrated Chelsea Hotel in New York City are very popular with long-stay visitors. A few hotels even have kitchens en suite with some of their rooms, so that you can prepare your own food, which is obviously much cheaper than eating out. Again, it may be worth considering such institutions as the YMCA and YWCA: in New York City, for instance, the 'Y' is open to both sexes and indeed functions as a normal (if somewhat basic) hotel, at very reasonable prices and with a high standard of cleanliness.

One other option which you may wish to consider is buying a motor-home and living in that while you are in the United States. Admittedly, this is more practical for an itinerant photographer or writer than for, say, an account-ant, but for many businesses, including import/export, it does have its possibilities. The only real difficulty, apart from the cost of the motor-home, is finding somewhere secure to park the thing while you are out of the country.

Visas, Taxes and Bureaucracy
The person who wants to work on both sides of the Atlantic is almost certain to be self-employed; few employers are

going to be prepared to ask for this on the one hand, or to tolerate it on the other. For visa purposes, much will depend on the sort of work you do. If your work is commissioned or sold in Britain, or if you are travelling on behalf of a business based in Britain and concerned with the export or import of goods or services between the UK and the US, a normal commercial non-resident visa (a B-1 visa) will be all that you need; these are not particularly difficult to obtain, and are subject to substantially the same requirements as non-resident non-business (visitors') B-2 visas. If you want to work *for an employer* in the United States, however, you will require some form of employment visa or else a Green Card, both of which are much harder to get (see Chapters 6 and 14). An employment visa will limit you to working for a single named employer, while a Green Card confers upon you many of the rights of an American citizen, with the notable exception of the right to vote, but also imposes upon you most of the duties of an American citizen *including military service*, though at the time of writing, the draft was in abeyance.

As described in Chapter 10, there are treaties which stop you being taxed twice (once by each country) on the same income, but this does not stop both Uncle Sam and Her Majesty's tax collectors trying to lay claim to your money; your difficulty is going to be trying to persuade one of them that the other is lawfully getting it.

As a general rule, you will be taxed in the country in which you spend the majority of your time, but even this is a matter for dispute: at the time of writing, the IRS would regard you as being resident in the US for taxation purposes under their 'substantial presence' test if you spent more than 31 days in the US in the current calendar year *and* 183 days during the current calendar year and the two preceding calendar years, though counting only a third the number of days in the first previous calendar year and an eighth the number of days in the second preceding calendar year – and the rules are different if you establish residency during that time. The best way to clarify this legalese is by means of an example. Supposing you spent 120 days in the US in 1986, you would count them in full. The 'first previous' year would then be 1985, and if you had spent 90 days in the country, you would count 'a third of the number of days', viz 30 days. The 'second previous' year would be 1984, and say 96 days in

1984 would count only as 12 days – one eighth of 96. The total would therefore be 90+30+12, or 132 days, which is 41 days less than the required 183 days. The whole subject is described at length in IRS Publication 518, *Foreign Workers, Scholars and Exchange Visitors*. The exact period may of course be varied by subsequent legislation. Otherwise, both countries will use 'intention' as the guideline in deciding which country gets your taxes, and as a typical indicator of 'intention' is the possession of a permanent base in a country, both may try to tax you if you have a permanent base in both. Deciding what constitutes a 'permanent base' is not easy, and you may rest assured that the tax authorities of both countries will give themselves the benefit of the doubt – which is another argument for hotels, a semi-formal arrangement with a family member or friend, or a motorhome.

Finally, US immigration laws are not really designed to cope with this sort of lifestyle: they cater for either the visitor or the immigrant, and with the best will in the world, they are not necessarily going to be able to handle transatlantic commuters easily. Theatrical commuters may be able to leave this matter in the hands of their agents, whilst in the United States there are actually immigration lawyers who specialise in the paperwork side of things: you may find it well worth your while to employ one of these, as all cases are treated as special cases and it is impossible to lay down general rules. Alternatively, you may adopt the Brer Rabbit approach (lie low and say nuffin'), which will usually work reasonably well if your visits are neither too long nor too frequent – two or three one-month visits a year, or a single visit of three months or so. For journalists, for example, such a low-profile approach is likely to be quite easy; for an importer/exporter, it may be more of a problem. A more detailed discussion of the types of visa applicable to different situations is given in Chapter 6.

Contract Work
In the aerospace and defence industries, in electronics, and in certain other specialised fields such as technical writing, there are surprisingly frequent opportunities for contract work in the United States, especially on the West Coast. If you are already committed to the lifestyle of contract work, this will need no further explanation; if you are not familiar

with it, a brief outline may be useful.

You are employed on local terms (which means American vacations – see Chapter 11) but at considerably better than average rates, typically 30–40 per cent higher than full-time employees. Your contract is (usually) for a fixed term, though open-ended contracts are sometimes encountered. The drawbacks are, first, that you have minimal security and, second, that you must be available to move at a few months' (or even weeks') notice to wherever the next contract is. Some people love the lifestyle; others simply cannot take it.

The formalities are usually taken care of by the employing company, who will advertise in the UK press, so it is an easy way of getting to live and work in the United States for a while, but you are unlikely to get the chance to visit the country first and to see if you are going to like it. It can also be very hard on families, which is why many people who do contract work are single, though many couples find it very exciting, even with children. You also have the advantage that your fares are normally paid both ways (though removal expenses may be minimal), and that you can travel between contracts – though during the period of the contract itself, your nose will usually be fairly firmly applied to the grindstone.

4

The Decision To Go

There are many reasons for deciding to spend some time in the United States, but they can be divided into three broad categories. There are the career advantages for an employed person; the entrepreneurial advantages for the self-employed; and, for everyone, there is the pure interest and excitement of working in a different culture, in a nation whose wealth and success (and shortcomings) are legendary.

For our purposes, career advantages include not only employment but also study. A curriculum vitae is usually improved by a touch of exoticism; it tells future employers that you are a person with initiative, someone who is adaptable and cosmopolitan, and someone who is not afraid to tackle something new. Working for your current employer in the United States seldom does your standing in his eyes any harm at all (unless he simply wants to get you out of the way – it does happen!), and when the time comes to change jobs it is guaranteed to pique a prospective new employer's interest. A stint of study at an American university or even an American school has the same effect; it makes you stand out from the crowd.

Admittedly, studying in the United States can be expensive, but there are many scholarships and grants available: your own university, college or even school may have exchange programmes and scholarships arranged with American institutions, and if they have not, they should be able to advise you about where to find out about such things. If you have children of school or university age, it is worth balancing the disruption of their British education against the potential benefits of an American education, as discussed in the next chapter and in Chapter 13.

The entrepreneurial advantages are also great, provided you choose the right field. Of course, working for yourself anywhere is likely to be very hard work, and adapting to a whole new set of trading conditions, commercial ethics and business law means that self-employment in the United States is likely to prove even more demanding than in the UK, so only you can judge whether it is worth while; but the authors number among their friends some people who have done it successfully, and who now enjoy a very much more interesting and expansive lifestyle than if they had stayed at home.

The third advantage, going abroad just for the fun of it, should not be underestimated. For most people, it will be something to do when they are young – perhaps in the gap between leaving school and going to college, or between leaving college and embarking on a career proper – because the spontaneity and freedom are much harder to sustain when you have children to consider, and the financial commitment is much greater. Couples without children, and without too many ties, may also consider it, but it must be something which both parties really want to do: if one loves America, and the other loathes it, it is a recipe for unhappiness and even divorce.

There are a surprising number of opportunities for short-term work in the United States, both legal and illegal, but if you want to return to the country, you will be well advised to stick to the legal ones. One of the best-known for young people is working at a children's summer camp (see Chapter 12), but there are various books about short-term work in the United States; a useful one is *Summer Employment Directory of the United States* (published annually by Vacation Work). Among the illegal ones (by which we mean working without a work permit, not working for the Mafia), summer harvesting work is one possibility and working in a bar or as a waiter or waitress is another; if you can sew, sweatshop owners in the garment districts of the major cities are notorious for not asking questions; and the possibilities of Alaska have already been mentioned. The authors also know people who have worked illegally as painters and decorators, as photographers and even as nannies; any employer who is prepared to hire you 'under the table' will do. It must be said, though, that the longer you do this, the riskier it becomes. Anything up to a year or so is comparatively easy, but after that, you start looking over your shoulder a lot, and unless you legalise your position by getting a visa which allows you to work and a social security number, acute paranoia can set in after a couple of years.

The main risk comes not from the Immigration and Naturalisation Service, who will usually only deport you, though
they may also refuse you subsequent entry, but from the
IRS, who take a very dim view of people who don't pay taxes.

However you go, it is worth trying to keep the duration of
your stay under your own control as far as possible.
Diplomats and armed-service personnel will only be able to
leave before the end of their allotted term of duty under
extraordinary circumstances, but most employers are more
flexible and will allow long-standing employees to leave
earlier for less pressing reasons; on the other hand, if you
are going to work for a new company, read the contract carefully. This is particularly true if they are paying removal
expenses and air fares, as they may not just refuse to pay
your return expenses, but also demand the return of your
expenses in moving to the United States, if you go home
unreasonably early. Most companies would regard anything
less than a couple of years, or at least eighteen months, as
unreasonably short; you can expect periods of homesickness, and periods when the whole country seems intolerable,
but at such times follow the counsel of Marcus Aurelius
Antoninus: consider what thou hast, and how thou wouldst
long for it if thou hadst it not.

A contract or assignment for a fixed period, with a renewal
clause, is best for both parties: an initial period of two or
three years is by no means unreasonable, and it may be
renewed annually thereafter or in longer tours. Some
companies will provide for home leave, either at your
expense or theirs, and others will not; again, this should be
in writing somewhere. Returning to the UK is more important to some people than to others, but if you have (for
example) elderly parents, you should be prepared and able,
both financially and by the terms of your contract, to return
to the UK, at least temporarily, as necessary. A open-ended
contract, where you are expected to stay in the United States
for as long as your company wishes, with the explicit or
unspoken implication that it will harm your career if you
return before they give you permission, can be a recipe for
very bad feelings indeed if you really do grow to dislike either
the country or the job itself.

As a Briton, you will enjoy many advantages in the United
States. From a practical point of view, the quality of the
British educational system is widely admired, and many

American employers feel that British employees add a bit of 'class' to their companies; in New York, a British secretary is a major status symbol. If your job involves dealing with people, you are automatically more memorable to your clients than an American would be, and this applies whether you are a merchant banker or selling used cars. The old showman's saying is that all publicity is good publicity, and your particular brand of foreignness provides you with first-class publicity without any need for gimmicks, though it does no harm to cultivate your Britishness. For example, driving a British car can be an excellent idea: a Jaguar, for example, confirms that you are British to the core and gives you a bit of pizzazz as well. Similarly, retaining a very British accent is well worth while, though you will inevitably find the occasional Americanism creeping in. A French friend of the authors said, when taxed with the fact that his Parisian accent was substantially unchanged after nearly a decade in the US, 'Of course. Ai worrk verry 'ard to keep zees accent!'

Although most Americans are tremendous Anglophiles, which includes the rest of the British Isles for their purposes, it is also true that there are some who are not. The only distinct anti-English groups, though, are likely to be unregenerate rednecks (especially in the South) and the American-Irish, many of whom are genuinely unaware that there are two sides to the Irish question. Even then, the innate willingness of most Americans to make friends with anyone will usually mean that although they may have a prejudice against English people in general, they will be unlikely to take against you personally.

On a more immediately practical level, the other drawbacks include ferocious immigration procedures, which are covered in Chapter 6; the much-publicised risks of mugging and murder, though these are usually exaggerated; the virtual absence of any kind of welfare net on the European model – not that potential welfare cases would be admitted anyway; and the absence or non-availability of many things which you take for granted in Britain.

Mugging and murder are very real risks in many places, as is rape, but equally, it is not particularly difficult to restrict oneself to places and situations where the risk is minimal. Between them, the authors have lived in the United States for about four decades, and they have yet to have a gun pointed at them there, and neither has ever been mugged, nor have they witnessed such events. On the other hand, we do not frequent the rougher parts of town, particularly at night; we stay in the central (patrolled) areas of New York subway stations; apart from our cameras, we do not carry anything obviously valuable with us; and if, for example, another motorist becomes abusive, we treat discretion as the better part of valour.

We have however both feared for our own safety on a couple of occasions, though nothing came of it, and we do have friends who have been held at gunpoint, two of whom were successfully robbed and the other of whom lay flat on the sidewalk as the guard at his hotel and his would-be assailant exchanged pistol fire over his head. In New York City, in particular, triple door-locks are the order of the day – but then, they are in Paris too, and they are becoming so in London. Like earthquakes in California, these are risks which you rapidly learn to live with, and besides, the authors know as many people who have been mugged in England, though admittedly not at gunpoint, as they know in the United States. American television cop shows create an impression of a more violent society than actually exists, and the American media tend to be more hysterical than the British, so although the true level of violence is greater than it is in Britain, it is far from disastrously so. It is also worth mentioning that the much-publicised murder rate in many American cities is often confined to certain neighbourhoods and certain socio-ethnic groups: in Los Angeles, for example, unless you are a member of a *barrio* street gang, or a drug dealer, the probability of your being shot is not all that much greater than in London.

On this topic, most Britons are fascinated by American gun laws: the right to keep and bear arms is something which they can hardly imagine. It is worth remembering that this is a freedom which we have only comparatively recently lost in this country – within the twentieth century – and that there is a good deal of truth in the slogan, 'If guns are outlawed, only outlaws will carry guns'. It is not difficult for a criminal to obtain a gun in Britain; by obtaining a gun for self-defence, the citizen becomes a criminal. The father of one of the authors owns several guns, and a number of shooting trophies; but he has never fired a shot in anger. 'I make no secret of the fact that I've got a gun,' he says, 'and maybe that's one of the reasons why I've never had any trouble.' Gun laws vary considerably from state to state, with the Eastern states imposing increasing restrictions while the Western states are less willing to do so. The NRA (National Rifle Association) fights strongly for the right to keep and bear arms, which is a symbol of American freedom – and given the rate at which freedom is being eaten up by federal and state law, it may well turn out to be the last American freedom to survive. As a symbol, it is hard to oppose; as a practical measure, it depends on whether you rate Freedom, with a capital 'F', over expedience and conformity.

This is also a good place to mention general American attitudes to police, justice, and law and order generally. Police forces vary widely in efficiency, politeness and honesty, but, with few exceptions, even the best of them are not up to the standards of most British forces. In general, though, the police respond well to a very British 'Excuse me, officer . . .', possibly because so few people are polite to them, and will be individually helpful; but many are extremely cynical about their jobs, and are convinced that all they can do in many areas is to provide a cosmetic service – making the streets *look* safe – rather than actually catching villains. Detection rates (in other words, the risk of being caught if you commit a crime) are much lower than in the UK, though it may surprise people to realise just how low even the British rate is: an average of 30–35 per cent, though, as a British police spokesman put it, 'Obviously we catch a higher percentage of murderers than that, but we may not do so well on motoring offences.'

There are also many kinds of police force. There are city and/or county police forces, much as in the UK, but there are also sheriffs' departments, State Troopers (state police), special highway forces such as the California Highway Patrol and of course the FBI (Federal Bureau of Investigation), which is normally only employed on serious federal (as distinct from state) cases. The division between federal and state law is sometimes confusing: murder is a state matter, for example, whereas taking women across state lines for immoral purposes is, perhaps inevitably, a federal crime, though it may well be the local police who deal with it, if it is dealt with at all. Of all the police, the Feds are the most feared, and the most rarely encountered, and sheriffs' departments are the most variable, because sheriffs are normally elected. Some are above reproach; others are distinctly 'open to offers'. The level of corruption in many police departments is probably a good deal higher in the US than in Britain, though as elsewhere it does not take many bent policemen to give the whole force a bad name.

Because the detection rate is so low, and because of America's puritan streak, penalties are in some cases savage to the point of meaninglessness, as well as very inconsistent: in California, where the average murderer serves less than ten years in prison, a man was sentenced in 1985 to 143 years for child molestation.

The actual administration of justice is similar in many ways to in the UK, with two exceptions. One is that many local judges are elected, rather than selected, from the ranks of the legal profession, so that their legal knowledge and consistency of sentencing may be less than satisfactory. The other is that corrupt judges undoubtedly exist. As a general rule, though, the higher and more senior a judge, the less the likelihood of corruption: the judges of the Federal Supreme Court (who are appointed, not elected) are as far above suspicion as any British High Court judge.

As for the welfare net, the United States immigration procedures are specifically designed to exclude anyone who might turn out to be a burden on the parish. Unemployment benefits are subject to much more rigorous exclusions than in the UK – they are never payable if you left your last job voluntarily, for example, or if you have been fired 'for cause', unless you can prove harassment or constructive dismissal – and they are payable for a limited period only, after which you go onto 'Welfare' (the US equivalent of British Social Security). Welfare will only just keep you from starvation, and is rigorously means-tested, though 'Social Security' (the American old-age pension) is not too bad and may be taken outside the United States. Social Security is, however, contributory and unless you have contributed for a substantial portion of your life, you will not be eligible. Likewise, 'Medicare' (the National Health Service division of Social Security) is only readily available to the elderly, though there are other recognised classes including the disabled and war veterans (special arrangements apply to the latter). A contributory disability scheme, which provides a disability pension, is operated by the state in most states, and by private insurers in others. As a general rule, private insurance is the only route to medical care, though there are charity hospitals for the genuinely poor.

Although most of our readers will not, we hope, be affected by any of this, there may well be other aspects of Britain which they will miss. One of the most obvious is the more generally relaxed attitude to work in Britain, but this is covered at greater length in Chapter 11. Apart from this, the things that you will miss tend to fall into two groups.

The first is those things which are specifically British, particularly British food and British television. One of the greatest mistakes which you can make abroad, in any country, is to try to live in exactly the same way as you did at home, because part of the time it will simply be impossible, and part of the time it will be prohibitively expensive. To take a trivial example, American bacon fries to a crispy, crumbly texture which is completely different from British bacon. Most people prefer the American variety, but if you set your heart on a British rasher, you are likely to be disappointed. Likewise, in the authors' view American bread is mostly so awful that it makes the worst sliced pap in Britain taste good, and speciality bakers are only slightly more common than hens' teeth. Thick cream is almost impossible to obtain – American thick cream is about as runny as British single cream – and if you have a weakness for Rose's lime juice, you will find that it costs anything up to three or four times as much for a bottle in the US as in the UK. These are merely examples which come immediately to mind; another is American meat. The beef is tender, but often contains alarming levels of hormones and is sometimes all but tasteless; pork is usually a good buy; but lamb is regarded as a fairly exotic meat in some places, and many Americans will not eat it because it is 'too gamey'! This explains why rack of lamb was *the* sophisticated dish of the early 1980s, but it also points up a lack of imagination in American cuisine which can be downright stifling in some areas – though in the big cities, and especially in New York and Los Angeles, there is a range of ethnic restaurants and shops which puts even London to shame, often in price as well as in variety.

The dear old BBC is something else which most people miss. Some radio stations in the big cities could almost compete with Radio Three when it comes to classical music, and the 'talk radio' and news channels more than make up for the lack of Radio Four; popular music is available from

41

innumerable stations, many of which specialise in particular styles such as hard rock, country-and-western, 'easy listening', or 'golden oldies', and beat Radio One hollow, but the advertisements are often intrusive, except on public-service radio.

Much more important than the loss of BBC radio, though, is the loss of British television. British TV has been described as 'the least worst in the world', and after a few hours of American TV you are likely to agree. Some BBC programmes do make it onto American TV, usually on the public-service channels; otherwise, the American network dream is the 'formula' which is beaten to death over years, or even decades, if it is successful. The idea of a British-style series, running over, say, thirteen weeks, with a detectable beginning, middle and end is utterly foreign to most American producers; the nearest they come is usually the 'mini-series' of three, four or five long episodes, such as *Shogun*. Many people resort to bootleg video copies of British TV programmes, but in order to indulge in this illegal activity you will need a video recorder and a television which can handle both the 625-line British PAL colour system and the 525-line American NTSC ('Never The Same Colour', according to some wags). Incidentally, most Americans are so impressed by British television that they even praise British advertisements, which are often better executed and almost invariably less intrusive than their American counterparts.

The second group of things which people miss are the ones which pertain to Britain's being a part of Europe. This is not just a question of buying cars which handle well – after all, these are imported both from Europe and from Japan – or of ethnic foods and the like, which are probably available somewhere at a price, but a matter of the more cosmopolitan outlook which any reasonably affluent person in Europe enjoys. For instance, in the US you can forget about going to Paris or Normandy for a long weekend, to Frankfurt for the book fair, or to Cologne for Photokina, unless you are very well-to-do: the sheer cost of the flight, and the time it takes to travel, rule it out. It is true that you can travel inside the United States, and that the American book fairs and the PMA show are world-class shows, but they still lack the cosmopolitan appeal which comes from visiting a different country, hearing a dozen different languages, and being removed from your customary milieu. To be sure, Las Vegas is different from New York, but Paris is a lot more different from London or Harrogate.

There are actually two disadvantages here, disguised as one. Not only will you miss the stimulation and interest of readily available European travel, but your American colleagues may seem terribly provincial and even parochial, simply because they have not had the chance to compare other cultures and societies in the way that you have. All Americans pay lip service to Italian design, French cooking, German engineering and so forth, but in most cases they have not had the chance to experience these things in context, and in many cases they will not have experienced them at all, or (still worse) they will have experienced only an ersatz version: anyone who has only tried the American version of German food must find it hard to understand how so many Germans can be so fat and jolly. You may also find it irritating to discover how very little most Americans know of Europe. Their grasp of European geography and history is usually extremely shaky by comparison with the average European's knowledge of the United States, and Americans tend to lump the whole of Europe together for the purposes of generalisations, though some do distinguish between Britain and The Rest. (In all fairness, Europeans often do the same for America, as witness the present generalisation!)

Once again, the impact of this will vary enormously according to where you are: New York is fairly cosmopolitan, though less so than you might expect, except among the upper reaches of society, and Los Angeles is not too limited, but in most other cities even the upper echelons of a company will contain few who have any more experience of Europe than one or perhaps two brief vacations.

You may also find the American attitude towards alcohol severely limiting; this has been mentioned before and will be mentioned again. In more and more states, the drinking age is being raised to twenty-one, though nineteen-year-olds may be allowed to drink 'three-two' beer (3.2 per cent alcohol or less). If your are under twenty-one yourself, or if you have children who are used to a drink in Britain, you may find this very irksome; and the fact that it is illegal to drink in a public place in most states actually makes a picnic with a bottle of wine technically illegal, though the police will seldom roust you for it. If you regard beer as no more than a harmless thirst-quenching drink, which is about all that weak American beer is good for, you may find it extremely irritating that you cannot drink a beer in the street, and that drinking a beer in your car if you stop for a roadside snack can land you in jail. Most American bars are definite dives, with expensive weak beer sold in small glasses, and the few that are reasonably pleasant to be in are usually attached to restaurants and charge even more for their liquor; there are also a few 'cocktail bars', which are reasonably congenial. Quite a few places call themselves 'pubs' in the United States, but few would attract any custom in Britain.

Despite all these disadvantages, there are many compensating advantages, and these should become more obvious as you read on. For example, in the big cities the shops stay open till eight or ten every night as well as opening on Sundays, while many grocery stores are open twenty-four hours a day. You can buy Californian wines, especially at the cheaper end of the market, which put their French equivalents to shame on both quality and price. Very high salaries mean that you can live handsomely on American goods, while even imports are more affordable than they look: Perrier water may be twice the price that it is in England, but if your salary is twice as much to boot, what is the loss? American manufactured goods, such as cars, household appliances and the like, are seldom in the forefront of either design or technology, but they are usually excellent value for money, and very reliable. Even so, when making your mind up to go to America for anything more than a few months, it is as well to have the disadvantages at the front of your mind, rather than the advantages, because after a while the advantages will become accepted as the norm, while the drawbacks will continue to rankle.

One more factor which must weigh heavily in your mind when deciding whether or not to go is keeping in touch with home. This is much more important to some people than to others, because some families can cheerfully go without seeing one another for years at a time, while others need family reunions every few months. The means of keeping in contact can be divided into a number of categories.

To begin with, there is the question of keeping generally in touch with British affairs and concerns. To some people, this is so important that they buy a British newspaper every day and read it avidly; British papers normally arrive a day late in major cities, several days late and to special order only out in the country. Others find that they can keep adequately abreast of British affairs by means of American newspapers and television, occasionally supplemented by a British magazine or newspaper, and letters and telephone conversations with home; this is probably a more realistic approach, as few people are going to be in a position to influence affairs in Britain anyway, and a relaxed attitude is no bad thing. As already mentioned, some people also like to receive video-cassettes of British television programmes; this is illegal (unless the video is an officially issued one) because it infringes copyright, but there is little likelihood of prosecution if the tapes are made by family or friends rather than commercially. You will, as already mentioned, need a dual-standard video recorder and TV set.

Secondly, there is the matter of keeping in touch with specific people at home. The American post office does not have a reputation for great efficiency, but the majority of letters do get through, and transatlantic telephone calls can be surprisingly cheap. Sending parcels is rather more of a problem, because airmail rates are very high, sea-mail takes forever and customs may take an unhealthy interest in either. Fresh or perishable foodstuffs should never be exchanged, both because of the likelihood of damage and because they will often contravene customs regulations, and valuables are best not sent through the mail because of the risk of loss and because duty may be payable. The best presents to exchange are either token gifts of little intrinsic value or very personal goods such as clothes, which have little resale value.

Ideally, of course, you will want to see people from home. This means that either you or they will have to cross the Atlantic, and it is worth bearing in mind the old adage that guests, like fish, stink after three days. Even family members are usually ill-advised to spend more than three or four weeks staying with one another, and for other friends a week or ten days is usually a realistic limit. You may be surprised at the number of people who can raise the air fare if they know that they can stay with you, but it is as well to make it clear, if that is the way that you feel, that while they are more than welcome to stay for a set period, which you should mention beforehand, you do not undertake to entertain or even necessarily to feed them while they are there; you might

45

also point out that they will need a car of their own, and suggest a cheap rental agency. Such arrangements are usually much more successful than those where the host feels under an obligation to show his or her guests around for the whole time that they are there, and a visit may safely be extended to two or three weeks or more. If you are a guest, you will appreciate the same courtesy.

There may of course be some people whom you wish to fly out at your own expense, usually parents or children, and hints on air fares are given in Chapter 7. The same goes for trips home, except that in the United States there is not quite the variety of 'bucket shops' and special deals that may be found in London.

Finally, there is invariably a strong temptation to form friends among the British expatriate community in your area, especially where there is a strong British presence (Los Angeles is a prime example) and there are things to be said both for and against this. On the one hand, it provides a ready pool of people with whom you have a certain amount in common, and from whom you can glean information about what is going on in Britain: there will always be somebody who has recently been home, or who has a British house-guest staying with them, or who has had some letter or received some tit-bit of news. On the other hand, expatriate communities can rapidly degenerate into gossip clubs where the main entertainment is damning America and all things American; this is particularly true when some of the members have too much time on their hands. There is also the risk that some people may begin to resent the 'British Mafia', and that you can harm both your social and your business life. It is far better to make a conscious effort to mix your friends as far as possible, with some fellow-Britons, some local Americans, and some Americans from other parts of the country.

It will be relevant to some of our readers to discuss at this point the problem of racism. As in any country, the impact of racism varies with your economic position, and a black lawyer or doctor will tend to be better received by his or her colleagues than a black store clerk or waiter or waitress. There is, however, no escaping the fact that black people are generally at a greater disadvantage in the South than in the North; the legendary racism of Alabama in particular survives to this day, and there are similar, albeit less acute, problems in the South as a whole. In the older and better-established non-industrial cities of the North, there may be a sizeable and well-to-do black population; in the industrial cities, such as Cleveland and Detroit, the position may be less comfortable. In the Midwest, there are very few black people, and while there is less overt racism than elsewhere east of the Rockies, you may feel conspicuous, though you may be more readily accepted if you are a member of an established church with a large following in the area.

Prejudice is probably least west of the Rockies; certainly, Los Angeles has plenty of prosperous black people (and plenty who are not so prosperous). It is also said that Alaska is a land of opportunity no matter what your colour, but you may well be mixing with some rough frontier types, so it is not something to gamble on.

Formerly, Japanese and Chinese were treated as 'California's Blacks', and there was overt (and sometimes legally codified) racial prejudice against Orientals, but this has substantially vanished since World War II – though the internment of Japanese Americans during that war remains a blot on the United States' history.

For Indians and others of similar racial type, there is generally little prejudice to contend with: except in the traditionally hard-core racist South, where anyone with a darker-than-Caucasian skin is liable to be called 'nigger', you are likely to be treated just as a white would be – which is usually a lot better than a North American 'Indian'.

As for those 'races' who do not think of themselves as such, several interesting phenomena arise. As a general rule, the British are very well liked, though the English themselves are often perplexed by references to 'your wunnerful English accent' being applied alike to public-school or BBC accents and Liverpudlian. Only in real redneck areas are you likely to hear the opinion growled that 'all limeys are fags' (homosexuals), but it does happen. The Scots are also well liked (though not clearly distinguished from the English by most people), and the American-Irish can be guaranteed to fall over themselves in an attempt to make someone from 'the ould country' welcome. Nobody seems to have heard of the Welsh, so unless you are prepared to grit your teeth and say that you're English, you will have some explaining to do.

5
The Family

The previous chapter focused on the individual's reasons for going to the US, but here we are concerned with the family's response, and with what their prospects are when they get there. For our purposes, 'family' can be divided into four groups: spouse, children, other dependants and pets.

Except perhaps for the pets, it is essential that everyone involved should be either enthusiastic about going abroad, or at least not actively hostile. This may sound obvious, but it is very easy for the main breadwinner to be carried away by the prospects of the New World, and to steamroller or try to steamroller the rest of the family's objections. Try to talk around doubts, objections and fears, and – unless you genuinely have no choice, as in an armed-services posting – try to remain open to the possibility of *not* going. Involve the children in the discussions as far as possible, and try to give fair weight to their wishes, but do not allow them to have the final word. You can expect, 'But I *hate* America!' from some children (some children *hate* everything) and a certain amount of opposition from teenagers, but usually the novelty of going to a country which they have only seen on television and movie screens will far outweigh the reservations – though coming back may be a different matter!

For short visits, even up to a few months, it may also be worth considering leaving the children behind, if they really do not want to go and if there are convenient grandparents, aunts and uncles, or whatever. If they are old enough, over sixteen say, you may even be willing to take the chance of letting them look after themselves; one of the authors knew a sixteen-year-old girl who lived on her own for nine months in her parents' house, while they were out of the country, without getting pregnant, turning into a drug addict, wrecking the place or otherwise giving them any cause for alarm. If you do leave children behind, though, make sure that they understand that they have had their opportunity,

School buses are widely used in the United States. They are invariably painted a bright 'gumball' yellow, and when they are stopped to load or unload children, they have ABSOLUTE priority: you must stop until the lights stop flashing and the bus moves away

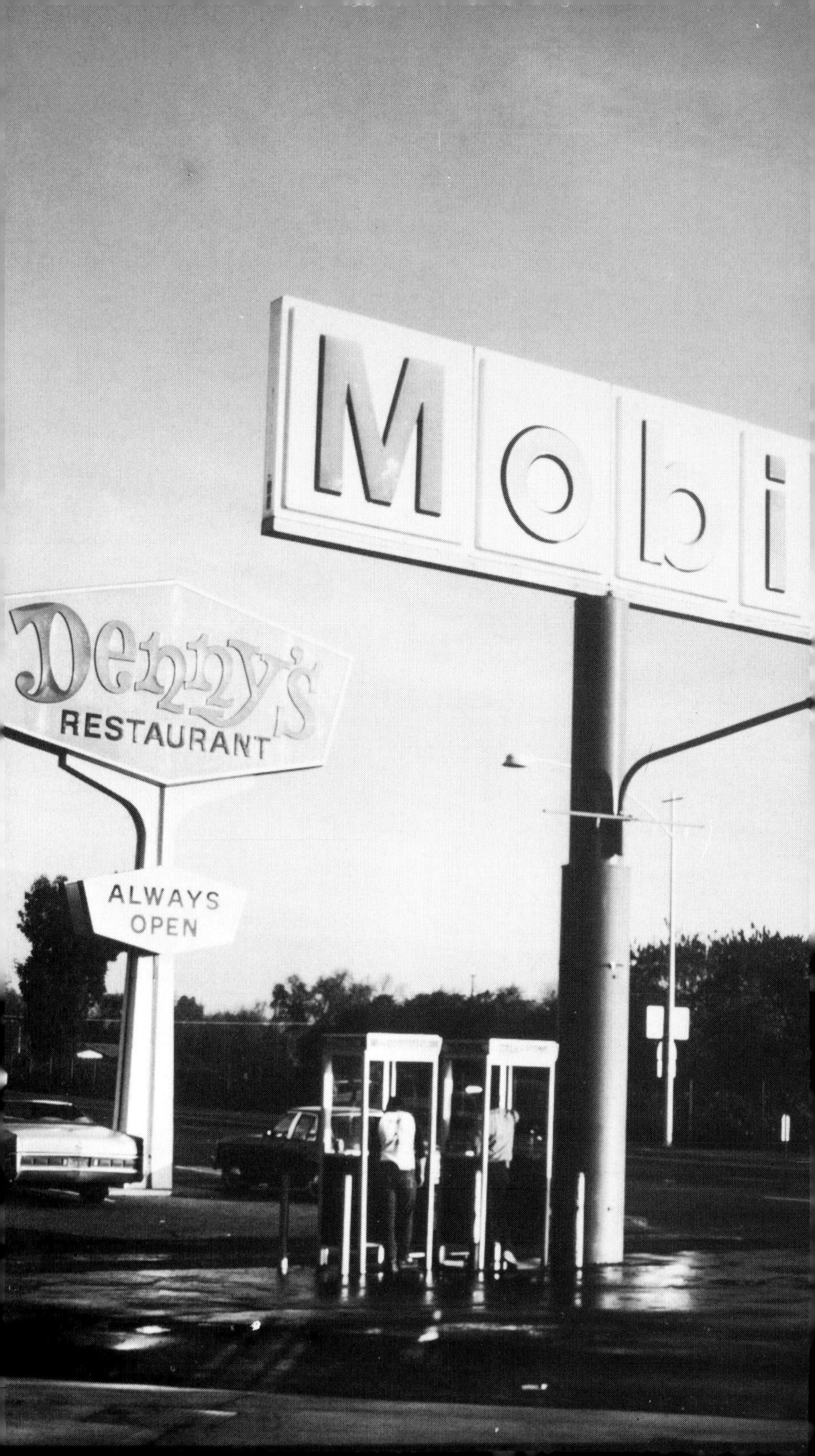
Mobi
Denny's
RESTAURANT
ALWAYS
OPEN

and blown it: place the responsibility squarely on their shoulders.

Leaving a spouse behind is another matter, and a fruitful source of trouble. Obviously it is a personal decision, but from observation of naval families, one of the authors is convinced that the divorce and separation rate among families who voluntarily separate like this is getting on for twice that of families who move together, though it is a matter for dispute whether this is cause or effect.

Assuming that you do take the family with you, it is important to consider their prospects in America. If, for example, your wife is rather shy, has always lived in the same area and likes to see her family for dinner every Friday night, you may be headed for serious problems: she may have built her few close friends up over years, even decades, and to tear her out of her familiar environment may change her considerably, for better, for worse, or simply for different – and you may not like the change. If at the other extreme she is outgoing, easygoing, and the child of, say, a navy man who was used to moving every two or three years throughout her childhood, she is unlikely to have any problems at all. History is not, however, an infallible guide: many an individual who was shy and nervous at home can blossom in a new environment, while others who were the life and soul of the party and pillars of the community can collapse when transplanted.

Even if you are not personally concerned one way or the other about a social life, you will receive plenty of social contact in the course of your work; but unless your spouse also works (which may not be easy – see below) he or she may simply languish at home. Given that not everyone wishes to work outside the house (or indeed is able to do so, if there are children to bring up), the availability of a social life is extremely important. A considerable danger in the United States is becoming a 'company man' (or woman) whose interests revolve solely around the company, with company-organised bowling and golf clubs, company-organised bridge clubs, dinner parties for other company people and their

(*left*) Public telephones are not as conspicuous in the USA as in the UK, but they are often to be found near gas (petrol) stations as well as in bars and public buildings. Tall signs, illuminated at night, are characteristic of most American towns but are even more widespread in the West than in the East

spouses, and so forth; as recently as the 1960s, these things were still regarded as the norm in many places, and failure to pull your weight in the company's social programme counted as much against you as failure to do your share at work. This is rapidly changing, it is true, and it has all but vanished among the newer companies, and in the West generally, but there is still enough of it about to bring some people (and especially their spouses) out in boils.

Fortunately, there are also increasing numbers of organisations which run entirely outside the company. Sports clubs and gymnasiums are an obvious example, and there are always general business clubs like the Rotary Club, the Kiwanis, and the Shriners, not to mention clubs with other aims, such as Mensa, which is particularly strong in America. Again, community theatre is very strong in many places, and although the standards are well above those of the typical amateur dramatics society in Britain, the people are likely to be welcoming and friendly; if you have any actual skills, such as lighting or scene-painting, you will be doubly welcome. Tenpin bowling is another place where couples can go together, and with the slightest effort meet new people. In practice, the natural friendliness of many Americans is such that a chance remark can rapidly develop into a friendship, or at least be given the opportunity of doing so: the British half of the authorship duo met people in camera stores, at Marineland, and (all the time) through friends-of-friends. Americans have a tremendous penchant for introducing their friends (even new-found friends) to one another and, as Britons, you and your family will almost automatically be regarded as people worth befriending.

Despite the old saw about 'a big city being the loneliest place in the world', the simple truth in the United States is that unless you like *really* small-town life, where everyone knows everyone else's business, the big cities are much easier places to make friends, because there are so many more places to meet people. Even introducing yourself to the people at the next table in a restaurant is unlikely to meet with a rebuff (unless they are lovers trying to enjoy a romantic evening!), because so many Americans are intrigued to meet British people; more than once, the authors have had people come over and talk to them in a restaurant, because they heard the accent and wondered where we came from.

The one place for making friends which you may well miss, though, is pubs: with the exception of 'singles bars' and 'gay bars', which people go to with the express intention of picking someone up or being picked up, people in American bars are usually more concerned with the serious business of drinking. Just occasionally, though, you will find magnificent exceptions: MacSorley's Old Ale House in New York City, for example, is a place where anyone could make friends – provided he is a man. They used not to allow women in at all, and even after they were compelled to do so by law, they did not go out of their way to make them welcome.

There are some more reflections on the status of women, and on men's social clubs (which are often rather childish) in Chapter 12, but one more point which is worth making here is that if you acquire an American spouse, you do not automatically acquire the right to stay in the United States, though you do receive a form of 'preferential status' which is so preferential that you really need to have a distinctly poor record before you will be refused a Green Card (see Chapter 14).

Employment opportunities for non-American spouses, on the other hand, may not be particularly impressive. In theory, for most visa types, your spouse has to go through all the same rigmarole that you do (see Chapter 6) in order to get a work permit, though in practice it tends to be easier for him or her to get one after you have done all the main work in establishing your credentials; and if you have an E-1 visa (see Chapter 6 again), your spouse is entitled to work without further paperwork. Nevertheless, American employers are inclined to be very cautious indeed, often to the point of xenophobia, and lack of American experience and American qualifications may well mean that your spouse is simply unable to work in his or her chosen field, or at least to work at the kind of level to which he or she was accustomed at home. Increasingly, a college degree is required (of which more later, when considering children's education), and even then additional restrictions may be applied, so that, for example, teachers are not eligible to teach without state accreditation, which may be automatically granted to teachers from other states but not to teachers from other countries unless they hold degrees.

Moving on to children, the image of the average American

child as a spoiled brat is often regrettably close to the truth. Side-by-side comparison of American and British children invites the conclusion that *as a rule*, British children are better behaved, more polite, less self-centred, less given to tantrums and sulks, and considerably more civil to their parents than American children. To a considerable extent, all this is a result of increased material wealth – the children, like their parents, genuinely *are* used to getting a great deal of what they want, when they want it – but the American media must take a share of the blame, because this is the image (mixed with a large dollop of precocity) which they present of American children, and which people therefore accept as normal.

There is also little doubt that some of this will rub off on your children, though it will take many years for it to become particularly deep-rooted, because your attitudes as a British parent are different and because your children will already have absorbed a fair amount of Britishness even without realising it, unless of course they are mere babes-in-arms when you take them to America. It is very hard to steer a course between excessive strictness (and any strictness will appear excessive when compared with the attitudes of some of your children's friends' parents) and simply giving in to everything they ask for.

If your children are of the right age, you will also run into the spectacular American schizophrenia on adolescents and sex. On the one hand, flirtatiousness and precocity are encouraged because they are 'cute', and boys and girls are encouraged to start dating at an absurdly early age: eleven or twelve is not regarded as unusual, and at Junior High School dances (the famous 'Promenades') both sexes are dressed and encouraged to behave like 1930s matinee idols. Then, when a *real* interest in sex sets in at puberty, society throws up its hands in shock and wails about the depravity of modern youth.

Obviously, *mores* vary widely from place to place, and what happens at Hollywood High will not happen in small-town Kansas, but in many parts of Los Angeles, for example, a seventeen-year-old virgin is something of a rarity, and many teenagers start sleeping together when they are sixteen, fifteen or even fourteen. This is admittedly not very different from what happens in the UK, but the difference is that the age of consent in California is eighteen, and that the offence known in Britain as USI (Unlawful Sexual Intercourse) is called in the US 'statutory rape' — 'statutory' because it is 'rape' whether the victim consents or not. Prosecutions are rare, especially when both parties are of similar age, but they are possible, and the penalties can be severe even when the seventeen-year-old 'victim' tearfully proclaims that the last thing she wants is for her boyfriend to be incarcerated; this is the classic revenge of the outraged father. The age of consent varies from state to state; at some times, in some states, it has been no less than twenty-one.

Paradoxically, the minimum age for *marriage* is much lower in many states than in the UK; marriage and intercourse outside marriage are separated in a way which would not occur to most people in Britain. In many states, the old ecclesiastical age limits of fourteen for boys and twelve for girls still apply, and in one of the southern states, it used to be as low as ten! Teenage marriages, especially with very young teenagers, are nothing like as common as they used to be, and most are voidable for lack of parental consent, but they are rarely automatically void for that reason.

It is to be hoped, though, you will be more concerned with your children's education than with their sex lives, and the American educational system is described more fully in Chapter 13. Having read this chapter, you may well feel that boarding the children in England is a better idea, especially if your company is prepared to foot part or all of the bill. The same is even more true if they are of university age.

As for other dependants, the operative word here is *dependants*. It is always comparatively easy to get a visa for someone who is not going to work, or at least, who is not going to take paid employment; and if you want to have your aged mother or your younger brother with you, then the Visa Department of the US Embassy is likely to look very favourably upon them if it is clear that you are simply their provider and benefactor. If, on the other hand, they suspect that you are trying to sneak someone in so that they can get a job in the US, they are almost certain to veto the application, or to insist that the 'dependant' in question goes through all the same paperwork that you yourself have done. Furthermore, although dependent children are exempt from some of the requirements for a Green Card (see the next chapter), such as blood tests, other adults are not, so the time and effort involved is altogether greater.

Finally, the cheapest way to ship pets to the US is as accompanied baggage (they will travel in the pressurised part of the aircraft's hold). You must provide them with a suitable airline-approved cage, though a few airlines may hire these out. Britain is a rabies-free area, so you will not be required to produce evidence of vaccination against rabies – though you will need to have the animals vaccinated for their own and for your protection. Only if you are planning a really long visit, at least a year, is it worth taking your animals with you: otherwise, the expense and inconvenience of quarantine on your return (see Chapter 15) will be considerable. It is, however, well worth taking your favourite animals with you on a long trip, as they will make it easier for you to adjust to the new environment, and often very much easier for your children. Apart from the rabies vaccinations, moving house internationally with a pet is very much the same as moving within the UK: there is no need for any other special precautions. Dogs in the United States are required to be licensed annually, just as in the UK, but the licence fee is rather higher, and there is usually a discount if the animal is neutered. In order to get a licence, you will need to produce evidence of rabies vaccination.

These remarks apply only to cats and dogs, however. Very small pets, such as mice and hamsters, are likely to prove prohibitively expensive to fly out and in any case may not survive the flight. Exotic pets, such as snakes and monkeys, may be subject to special restrictions or even prohibitions, so check with the American Embassy before you leave.

6

Visas

In order to enter the United States at all, at least legally, you need a visa. There is a bewildering variety of types of visa, and both the types of visa and the requirements for their issue may be changed at any time, but this chapter accurately reflects the law which was in operation in 1985. In case of difficulty, the relevant document is the booklet *United States Immigration Laws: General Information*, issued by the Immigration and Naturalisation Service of the United States Department of Justice and available from the Embassy (see Appendix 2) on request: the reference number on the cover is M-50.

The broadest and most obvious division of visa types is into non-immigrant and immigrant. Although this book is not primarily intended for immigrants to the US, an 'immigrant' visa may be required if you want to change jobs freely within the US, and will certainly be required if you wish to extend your stay indefinitely. Non-immigrant visas are covered first; immigrant visas are covered in the second part of the chapter.

Non-Immigrant Visas

There are twelve types of non-immigrant visa, each designated by a letter of the alphabet, and although the alphabetical order does not reflect the frequency of issue or the likely usefulness to our readers, it is easier to stick to it for ease of reference. In all of them, unless otherwise stated, the period is not defined, being at the discretion of the immigration officer at the port of entry, and the visitor must have no intention of abandoning his or her residence outside the United States. Your passport should also have six months to run *after* the end of your stay: this is to ensure that you will be allowed back into your own country when you leave the US. Certain types of visas are issued only on the basis of reciprocity; in other words, unless the applicant's government issues similar visas (or visas which allow similar privileges to similar people), the US Government will not issue them. This is not a problem with UK citizens.

There is also a distinction between visas for which a *visa petition* is required, and those for which it is not. A visa petition establishes preferential or immediate-relative status and must be approved by the Immigration and Naturalisation Service and received by a consular officer. Visas for which a petition is required are marked with an asterisk below. For relatives, the relative files the petition; for the professions, or 'exceptional ability', anyone can file; and for H-2, H-3 and L visas, the 'intending employing party' must file. Further information on immigrant visa petitions is given at the end of the chapter.

All applicants for visas must satisfy certain conditions. As the booklet mentioned above puts it, 'In short, aliens who do not measure up to the moral, mental, physical and other standards fixed by law are, with few exceptions, excludable from admission even if they have the necessary documents.' This is understandable in most cases, but considering the ease with which American citizens can enter most European countries, the impositions of the B-2 (tourist) visa may seem like a damnable cheek. Some of the conditions which may lead to exclusion include mental or physical disability or unfitness; illiteracy; chronic alcoholism and drug addiction; or being one of 'those who are, or have been, members of or affiliated with any organisation that advocates or teaches the overthrow, by force or violence or other unconstitutional means, of the Government of the United States or of all forms of law'.

Type A visas are for diplomats of various types, and 'certain other accredited and accepted officials and employees of recognised foreign governments' and their immediate families.

Type B visas are the most usual. They are issued to those who are visiting the United States temporarily for business or pleasure, and do not cover other family members unless they are shown on the same passport *and* the 's' in 'bearer(s)' in the visa itself is not deleted. B-1 visas are issued for business, B-2 for pleasure.

Type C visas are transit visas for 'immediate and continuous transit through the United States', with the interesting provision that they also cover transit to and from the United Nations Headquarters District.

Type D visas are for members of the crew of ships and aircraft, who intend to leave with their ship or aircraft or with another ship or aircraft after a temporary stay in the United States.

Type E visas are issued to a person entering the United States 'solely to carry on substantial trade between the United States and the foreign state of which he/she is a national, or solely to develop and direct an enterprise in which the alien has invested or is actively in the process of investing a substantial amount of capital'; spouses and unmarried children under twenty-one are also entitled to the same kind of visa *and are entitled to work in the US*. Type E visas are one of the most flexible varieties available, and are sometimes used for contract workers (see Chapter 3); in this case, the prospective employer will help with the visa.

Type F visas are issued to students (and their spouses and unmarried children under twenty-one) intending to 'pursue a full course of study at an established institution of learning or other recognised place of study'.

Type G visas are diplomatic again, but are for the 'designated principal resident representative' of a recognised foreign government, whereas Type As are for career diplomats etc, only. These visas also cover representatives of or to international organisations, including the UN. Not only members of the immediate family are covered, but also 'attendants and servants'.

Type H* visas are particularly interesting. They are in three categories. First, there are visas for those 'of distinguished merit and ability' going to the US 'to perform services of an exceptional nature', though doctors of medicine (defined as 'a graduate of a medical school') may also teach and conduct research at public or non-profit institutions or agencies. Secondly, an H visa may be issued to someone who is coming temporarily to perform temporary services or labour, if unemployed persons capable of performing such services cannot be found in the US, though this clause does not apply to graduates of medical schools going to the US to perform services as members of the medical profession. Thirdly, they cover trainees in various fields, but excluding (once again) graduate medical training or education, together with their spouses and unmarried children under twenty-one.

Type I visas are issued to bona fide representatives of 'foreign press, radio, film, or other foreign information media', plus their spouses and unmarried children under twenty-one.

Type J visas are for a 'bona fide student, scholar, trainee, teacher, professor, research assistant, specialist, or leader in a field of specialised knowledge or skill, who seeks to enter the United States temporarily as *a participant in a program designated by the Secretary of State*'. This time, medical people are specifically included.

Type K* visas are fiancée or fiancé visas for those who are going to marry a US citizen within ninety days after entry, together with the fiancée or fiancé's unmarried children under twenty-one. Unless the marriage takes place within ninety days, the holders of K visas are required to leave, *and there is no provision either for extending the visa period or for getting another type of visa*, but if the marriage does take place, they 'shall be recorded as permanent residents'.

Type L* visas may again be of particular interest to our readers, as they are for intracompany transferees who shall, immediately preceding the time of application for admission into the US, have been employed continuously for one year by a firm, corporation, etc, and who seek to enter the US temporarily in order to work for the same employer or a subsidiary or affiliate, in a capacity that is managerial, executive or involving specialised knowledge. Spouses and unmarried children under twenty-one are once again included, but (as in the case of most types of visa) may not accept paid employment without work visas of their own.

All visa holders are required to stay in the US *only* under the conditions of their own visa, but the position of students is particularly hedged about with restrictions. The place of study must be designated in advance by the would-be student, and approved in advance by the attorney general, and no change of school or college is permitted without consent of the Immigration and Naturalisation Service. Work (even temporary work) is not permitted unless the student can show that it is necessary in order to maintain the student as a student, *and* that the necessity arose due to unforeseen circumstances arising after acquisition of student status, though employment for practical training may be permitted where it is recommended by the school being attended and where it is unavailable in the student's country of residence. A student's spouse or children may not accept any gainful employment as long as they hold an F visa.

Visas other than C, D and K may be extended if the visitor's status is unchanged and if the period of admission originally specified has not expired. Applications for extension must be made not more than thirty days nor less than fifteen days before the expiry of the original term, and the applicant must show that he or she has acted 'in good faith', so steadily slipping the leaving date is not possible.

The documentation required to support an application for a non-immigrant visa will vary according to the type of visa required, and according to the issuing office's opinion of the likelihood of your becoming an illegal immigrant, but you should be prepared to support your application with proof that you intend to return to the UK; single men are viewed with particular suspicion. You will be notified of the paperwork, if any, which is required in addition to your passport when you make your visa application, but for tourist (B-2) visas you will normally need the following:

1. A visa form ('Optional form 156');
2. A recent photograph 1½in square with your usual signature written on the *reverse* side;
3. 'Evidence substantiating the purpose of your trip and your intention to depart from the United States after a temporary visit'.

Optional form 156 provides various suggestions concerning the last requirement, including a letter from your employer for business trips, or for pleasure trips 'documents outlining your plans while in the US and explaining the reasons why you would return abroad after a short stay, such as family ties, employment, or similar binding obligations in your home country'. Freelances can have a problem here: evidence of house ownership and of UK contracts are one possibility, and a letter from your bank manager or from someone for whom you work regularly is another. This whole provision is your first intimation that the United States is not *quite* such a free country as it likes to paint itself.

Type B visas may be applied for by mail, which can take a month or even longer, or in person at the American Embassy, which normally takes at least three hours but is at least a same-day service. Several recorded information services are available at the Embassy; at the time of writing, the main number was 01-499 3443, and requests for written information could be left on 01-499 7895.

With the exception of B visas, most of the other classes of visa which are likely to interest our readers will normally be handled to a considerable extent by someone else, usually an employer or prospective employer (A, G, H-2, H-3, most I, and L). Applicants for K visas will either be acquainted with the country, or (by definition) have someone in the US to help them. Applications for C and D visas are little more demanding than for B visas; E visas, and I visas for freelances, are normally special cases, and are handled as such; applicants for F and J visas may be able to get help either from their British educational establishment or from their prospective American school (college); and the burden is on H-1 applicants (or their employers or prospective employers) to prove that they meet the requirements of the visa.

From all of the above, it will be clear that it is virtually impossible to go over 'on spec' to look for work in the United States, although, of course, it may be possible to look for work on a vacation and to persuade a prospective employer to support your application for an H-2 visa, though these are not easily granted; an immigrant visa may be more appropriate. This is also likely to be the case if you want to change jobs in the US, because if you go over with your present employer, you will go in on an L visa, and changing jobs would involve a change in status. Likewise, the self-employed who are not eligible for non-immigrant E visas may well need immigrant visas. Academics are well placed, however, thanks to category J, though the American secretary of state's attitude can vary widely from administration to administration on this point.

Perhaps the most awkward aspect of all, when dealing with American visas, is that the decision as to whether or not you are admitted to the United States rests finally with the immigration officer at the port of entry, and that he or she is entitled to turn you back, though they will not usually do so lightly. If you have plenty of money, in cash or traveller's cheques, and a return ticket to the UK, a visit of up to three or even six months is unlikely to be queried, though if you have a bank account is the United States, this may actually count against you. A lot will also depend on your port of entry: Californian immigration officers are notoriously sticky, while those on the East Coast are less inclined to view you as a potential illegal immigrant. Entry via the Canadian border is particularly easy, as passports are not necessarily checked at all.

Immigrant Visas

There are effectively five categories of immigrant into the United States. These are refugees; special immigrants; immediate relatives of US citizens or resident aliens; aliens who meet the requirements of a 'preference category'; and those who enjoy no preferential status.

Refugees require no further explanation, except to say that they have no *automatic* right of entry, and that although there may be numerical limits enforced from time to time (50,000 in 1982, for example), there is basically no quota. *'Special immigrants'* is a rag-bag category, again without numerical limitation, covering former citizens reapplying for citizenship, non-citizen lawful immigrants returning from a temporary visit abroad, ministers of religion (and their spouses and unmarried children under twenty-one) who have no other occupation and whose services are 'needed' by their churches in the US, and employees or honourably retired employees of the US Government abroad, with at least fifteen years' service. The last is only available in 'exceptional circumstances'.

'Immediate relatives' include the children, spouse and parents of a US citizen, and these are again admitted without numerical limitation. There are various restrictions – a citizen who wishes to bring in a parent must be at least twenty-one, for example; children must be under twenty-one and unmarried; and children other than legitimate children are subject to additional and complicated (but usually easily met) requirements. The M-50 booklet explains all this.

Admission of other immigrants, both preference and non-preference, is subject to numerical restrictions – 270,000 annually, on the last figures available – with a ceiling of 20,000 for natives of any one foreign state. Within these limits, admissions are carved up as follows:

1. First Preference (20 per cent of total): sons or daughters of US citizens over twenty-one and/or married, ie those not coming under the 'Immediate Relatives' category.

2. Second Preference (26 per cent of total *plus* any not required for first preference): spouses and unmarried sons or daughters of permanent resident aliens.

3. Third Preference (10 per cent of total): members of the professions, or those who 'because of exceptional ability in the sciences or arts will substantially benefit prospectively the national economy, cultural interests, or welfare of the United States and whose services in the professions, sciences, or arts are sought by an employer in the United States'. As may be seen from the definition, the ability does not have to be all that exceptional.

4. Fourth Preference (10 per cent of the total, plus any not required for the first three preferences): married sons or daughters of US citizens.

5. Fifth Preference (24 per cent of total, plus any not required for the first four preferences): brothers or sisters of US citizens, provided the citizens in question are over 21.

6. Sixth Preference (10 per cent of total): those capable of performing skilled or unskilled labour, not of a temporary or seasonal nature, for which there is a shortage of employable and willing persons in the US. 'Labor certification' (see below) is required in this category.

After these six categories, non-preference immigrants will be admitted according to the chronological order in which they apply. As the above percentages add up to 100 per cent, non-preference immigrants can only get in if the preference categories are not filled, and spare places therefore exist. There are huge waiting lists for non-preferential immigrants, who must also provide 'labor certification', so it can take literally years to get in.

All immigrants must be 'qualified', that is to say, not excluded because of the aforementioned 'moral, mental, physical and other standards fixed by law' – and they need to prove it! Once you have your immigrant visa, you must normally go to the US within four months (less in some cases), at which time you will be admitted for 'permanent residence'. Immigrants over the age of fourteen are fingerprinted when they apply for immigrant visas, and those under fourteen must be fingerprinted within thirty days of their fourteenth birthday. Non-immigrants are also fingerprinted if they remain in the US for longer than one year *and* they are nationals of countries which require fingerprinting of US citizens temporarily residing therein (Britain does not).

Every alien eighteen years or older who is required to be registered must carry, at all times, a Certificate of Alien Registration or Alien Registration Receipt Card. 'Failure to do so may result in fine and imprisonment', as the official pamphlet puts it. Changes of address must be filed within ten days of such change, and aliens who are temporarily in the US must report their addresses to the Immigration and Naturalisation Service every three months whether they have moved or not; failure to do so can result in a fine, imprisonment or deportation. At this point, 'Land of the Free' begins to sound rather a grotesquely implausible description.

From this, it will be clear that getting into the United States is not easy unless you are an immediate relative of a US citizen. Even if you enjoy that status, the immigration procedure is difficult, time-consuming, and indeed arrogantly administered: the British half of the authorship duo has never completed an application for immigrant status, because it was simply not worth the effort *or the expense*; it cost well over $100 when he last checked, in the early 1980s, so the commuting option (Chapter 3) seemed more appropriate. A description of the requirements which he would have to meet will show how this is so; bear in mind that unless you marry a US citizen, or unless you can get an employer to back you under the third preference, you will have even more to do.

In order to get an immigrant visa, you must first file a visa petition. This begins with a Form 222, 'Preliminary Questionnaire to Determine Immigrant Status', which is a comparatively simple form to determine whether you fall within a preferred group.

On the basis of this form, the US Embassy will tell you what other forms and documents are needed – at the very least, birth certificates for yourself and your spouse and children if applicable, and passport(s). They will send you a longer and more probing form to fill in, and in the case of 'immediate relatives', the relative must fill in a form and provide proof of relationship, swear that you are related and pay a fee: for a third-preference visa, the employer will have to do something similar. If you have *any* convictions for *any* offences, including motoring offences, you must furnish official court records, or a letter from the court, giving details of the offence and the penalty imposed; digging up records of a motoring offence in your youth can be difficult, the more so as the British courts are often not equipped to furnish the information, and cannot understand why you want it anyway.

You will also need to prove to the satisfaction of the consular officer that you are unlikely to become a 'public charge'. In order to do this, they require documentary evidence *in duplicate* that you have, or will have in the US, sufficient funds to provide for yourself and your family; or that you have employment waiting for you which will provide an adequate income; or that you are skilled in a profession or occupation which has been determined to be in short supply in the United States, and that you can not only afford to get over there, but also to keep yourself and your family until you find a job; or that someone in the US will 'assure' your support.

The actual form of proof will vary, but bank statements and a letter from the bank manager are one possibility; proof of ownership of real property or investments is another; proof of income from business investments or book royalties might be a third; and so on. If you have someone to 'assure' your support, they must provide evidence that they can afford to do so, such as notarised copies of their latest income-tax return, or evidence similar to that already listed for the applicant. There is no official form of affidavit, but at the time of writing the Embassy would supply a sample form (OF-167A) free of charge, attached to their general letter 'Optional Form 167', and it is easiest to use this.

Then, once you have submitted all the documents (which will vary from visa category to visa category), you will be called to make yourself available for *a full day* at the American Embassy, usually from 8.30 in the morning to

(*above right*) Although New York's Central Park, like many others throughout the country, is famed as the haunt of muggers and robbers, there are many smaller parks where you can walk in safety. This is Battery Park, on the south tip of Manhattan Island, in January; the temperature when this picture was taken was a fairly typical 15°F, −10°C

(*below right*) In the United States, as in the UK, old industrial and dockside areas are being renovated and turned into leisure and tourist attractions. This is Fisherman's Grotto, in San Francisco

5.30 in the evening, though the actual application may take less time. There, you will be interviewed by a consular officer, whose attitude may vary from the charming to the hostile, via the indifferent, and sent along for a medical examination *including a blood test for syphilis*. The United States is obsessed with syphilis, and even requires blood tests before marriage. If at the end of this day you are found eligible for an immigrant visa, one will be issued, and you will then have four months to get into the United States.

The whole procedure must be completed within specified time limits, which may be varied from time to time, or you will have to start all over again, including paying fees all over again.

(*left*) If you've got it, flaunt it . . . Rodeo Drive, Beverley Hills, is the Bond Street (or Rue Faubourg St Honore) of Los Angeles, and all the most expensive stores are in this area. There is less reticence about displaying wealth in the West than in the East, and the East is generally less reticent than the UK

LSA-E

7

Leaving
The United Kingdom

The American side of the paperwork has been dealt with already. From the British side, all you really need is your passport, though for short trips (up to a few months) you will also be well advised to take out holiday or business travel insurance, which covers cancellation of tickets, loss or theft of property, and (very importantly in the United States) medical insurance. Make sure that the medical insurance limit is realistic; nothing less than $100,000 can be considered truly comprehensive, and $1,000,000 is not out of the way. If you are self-employed or otherwise not on PAYE, you will need to settle your tax affairs if you are actually changing domicile. Otherwise, you will need to make decisions as to what to do about your house; about storing or transporting your household effects; and about transporting yourself, and your family across the Atlantic.

For anything less than three months, the only realistic thing to do with the house is to lock it up, entrust the key to a reliable neighbour, tell the police where you have gone, and hope for the best. Turning off the water is a good idea, but you can leave the refrigerator and freezer running for three months without any problems – though if there is a power failure, or if you have a surge trip-switch and it is activated, they will smell unbelievably unpleasant when you open them again.

Sometimes you may be able to find a 'house sitter' whom you can trust, or you may be able to arrange an exchange with an American family, whereby they use your house and you use theirs; several organisations exist to bring would-be exchangers into contact. Exchanges can also be arranged for longer periods: this is particularly true among academics, who may well be able to exchange jobs for a year, as well as houses.

For longer periods, locking up becomes an increasing risk, and many insurance companies will not cover a house which is unoccupied for more than a specified period, or sometimes for more than a specified number of days per year: read your policy carefully. The choices then become renting (or sub-letting if you do not own your house) and selling. If you live in rented accommodation, of course, the only sensible thing to do in most cases is to give it up if you are going to be away for more than a very few months.

Renting out your house has the twin advantages that you retain a base, and that you still have your investment in property in the UK in a fairly safe and high-yielding form, and that far from being a drain on your resources, it can actually be a source of income. The size of your mortgage will determine the excess (if any) of income over outgoings, but it is usual to rent a house exclusive of rates and utilities; if these are included, it is best to say so in the lease. Make sure that the utility companies realise that your tenant is liable for all bills, or they may try to pursue you. If you rent the house yourself, make sure that the terms of your lease allow you to sublet, and if you have a mortgage, check that its terms permit letting, though most building societies will agree if you explain the circumstances.

The drawback of renting out your house, on the other hand, is that you never know what your tenants are going to do to it. Even if you use a reputable agent, or rent via a large organisation (the armed services rent houses in many districts, and administer them well), there is still likely to be a fair amount of wear and tear, and if you are unlucky it can amount to actual damage. Furthermore, when you return, you have to get the tenants out of the house. Once again, a reputable agent can save a lot of trouble here, but it is by no means impossible that your tenants will be unwilling to leave, and that it will take you anything up to several months – during which time you are unlikely to be receiving any rent – to get them out. And finally, you realise no capital if you rent your house out rather than selling it, though this is unlikely to be a problem unless you are contemplating a *really* long stay in the United States and believe that it would be worth your while to buy a place there: this is dealt with in more detail in the next chapter.

Selling removes all these worries, and allows you to put your money into a reliable high-yield security which will

71

usually offer little (or no) less return than the capital appreciation of the house. It also stops you having to worry about accounting for the income from the house to both the Inland Revenue and the IRS. On the other hand, you will lose the tax advantages which you enjoy on your mortgage (provided you can still persuade the Revenue that it is still your 'principal dwelling' and that you intend to return there), and if house prices suddenly increase dramatically, as happens from time to time, you can find that you have been knocked several rungs down the house-buying ladder, and may indeed have fallen off it altogether.

Whether you sell or rent, you are unlikely to want to leave your house fully furnished with all your own trinkets, knick-knacks, and objets d'art. At most, you will want to leave only basic furniture in a rented house (renting out unfurnished accommodation in Britain is unwise, because of rent controls and the increased difficulty of removing unwanted tenants); so you are going to be faced with transporting, storing or disposing of many of your worldly goods. Even if you already have plenty of experience at moving house within the UK, you will find that international moving is a rather different proposition.

A major consideration is who is paying to have your goods shipped. If your company is doing it, they may be prepared to cover furniture and everything else, or they may set a limit either on space or on price; or again, they may pay a percentage of your moving expenses, with or without limit, leaving you to cover the rest. It is important to be sure exactly what they will and will not pay for – including professional packing, as well as the cost of shipping – and it may also be relevant whether they will pay in advance or in arrears. They may also have preferred companies, so find out before you get the quotes. If you are paying yourself, it is as well to be very selective. Another important consideration is who will be paying to bring your belongings back when you return!

Whoever is paying, it is always a good idea to get three different quotes from three different companies. Most removal companies will quote for nothing, but make sure that you are comparing like with like: packing (or not), insurance, delivery dates *to your door* and unpacking (or not). Even among reputable companies, quotations may vary widely, sometimes by a factor of two or even three to one.

Usually, the *minimum* quantity which may be shipped is 500lb (227kg), so even those who travel relatively light will be taking a fair bit, though it is surprising how quickly things can add up; the authors once flew a third of a ton of household goods home with them, as excess personal baggage. On some airlines, particularly on transatlantic routes, this approach can prove surprisingly cheap: each person is allowed two pieces of baggage, weighing up to 62lb (28kg), the combined dimensions of which (length + breadth + depth) must not exceed 62in (157cm). After this, excess baggage may be charged per piece (subject to the same size limitations) or by weight, depending on the airline. The latter is likely to prove prohibitive, but the former can be a bargain. Otherwise, shipping relatively small quantities (under 500lb/227kg) can be very expensive indeed.

The criteria to use in shipping must be a personal matter, but a few guidelines can be laid down. First, most UK electrical appliances will be substantially useless in the US unless they are specifically dual-voltage. The 110V 60Hz American supply is incompatible with the 240V 50Hz requirements of UK equipment, and even if you want to bother with transformers, the difference in mains frequency will mean that synchronous motors run 20 per cent fast. This is not critical with, say, a hair-dryer, but it does not do much for a record or tape deck. Curiously, some heavy-duty American household appliances such as cookers and driers do run at 220V or 240V (still at 60Hz) which is supplied on a separate household circuit, but these are hardly worth shipping from Britain, as American-made models are cheap and fit in better in an American kitchen or utility room. Conversely, they are usually far too big to ship back to Britain.

Secondly, everyday furniture is probably not worth shipping, as it can easily and cheaply be replaced in the United States – unless, of course, you have particularly fine pieces. This is especially true of antique or Victorian and Edwardian furniture, which is at a premium in the United States, and which will make your house the envy of your American friends, especially in the West. It is also true of first-quality modern furniture, which will cost a good deal more in the United States, so if your house is a showpiece of classic design you may decide to ship rather more. You should, however, be aware of the possible adverse effects of hot, dry climates on antique furniture: unless it is carefully maintained, with polish and (sometimes) furniture oil, there is a danger of splitting and cracking. In antique stores in California and the other Western states, you will occasionally hear a sound like a pistol shot as a piece of wood suddenly cracks in the dry air.

For most people, though, the important stuff to ship will fall into three categories. The first is personal clothing, though packing does provide an excellent opportunity for weeding out things you have not worn for years. The second is household goods such as sheets, pillowcases, blankets, kitchenware, cutlery, china and glass and so forth, which can add up to a surprising amount of money if you try to replace them all, and which are hardly worth storing. The sheer volume of this category is sometimes hard to believe: when you start thinking of trays, decanters, kitchen knives and whisks, you realise just how much there is. The third is personal accoutrements, which covers a surprising range of things, from household ornaments and favourite antiques through jewellery and cameras to books and papers. Unless you are one of those people who never accumulates anything, these are the things which place your personal stamp on a house, and which are too valuable either intrinsically or sentimentally to risk in store.

Even these three categories, without any furniture, can rapidly add up to a remarkable weight. Books in particular add up frighteningly quickly: any hardback weighs a pound or two, and a shelf of books can easily weigh ten or twenty pounds *per foot*. A tea-chest full of books is virtually immovable by a single person, which is a factor to bear in mind when packing!

Obviously your most valuable goods, particularly jewellery and cameras, will travel with you as carry-on baggage, but otherwise it is not unrealistic to allow 500–1,000lb (225–450kg) per adult person *even if you do not intend to take any furniture*.

The rest of your property will need to be sold or stored. The cost of storage can easily be established by obtaining quotations, and from there it is a relatively easy matter to decide whether to store or dispose of various items of furniture: if the cost of storage (including insurance) over the period that you are going to be away exceeds the value of the items to be stored, there is not much question about it. Be as ruthless as you can, but remember too that you will ultimately have to replace many of these things, and that prices will inevitably go up. Once again, much will depend on the value of what you store, but more people find upon their return that they have stored things they no longer want than find that they have got rid of too much.

It is also worth considering the possibility of storing goods in the US, particularly if your company is prepared to pay for shipping. That way, even if you have no accommodation lined up, or if you plan to stay in temporary accommodation while looking for a longer-term base, you will have your furniture and other effects handy when you do find somewhere. Although furniture depositories are more expensive in the US than in the UK, there is an alternative in the form of 'self-storage' or 'mini-storage' facilities. These are individual lock-ups, rather resembling blocks of garages, and typically range in size from about 4×5×6ft (120×150× 180cm) to 20×30×15ft (6×9×4.5m), with four or five sizes in between. The lock-ups themselves are inside a secure chain-link compound, and there will often be a resident caretaker. Mini-storage units are much cheaper than depositories, though not perhaps quite as secure (it is sometimes possible to force access from a neighbouring unit, so check construction carefully).

A topic which has not yet been mentioned is customs. If you have any particularly fine or valuable antiques, you will need export licences from the UK, though these are usually readily granted for private household goods. The definition of the types of antiques which fall under these provisions varies with the type of antiques, and very few people are likely to be affected, so it is not worth giving details here, but HM Customs and Excise will help. Your nearest office can be found in the telephone directory under the heading 'Customs and Excise'.

At the other end, US customs are very much a matter of luck. If you are obviously a temporary visitor, you can take in almost anything – but the definition of 'temporary' is up to the customs officer, as is the question of what he or she will allow. As a general rule, bona fide used household goods and personal clothes and effects will be allowed in without impost; furniture will not usually be assessed, unless it is particularly valuable; and personal valuables such as jewellery and cameras are unlikely to be taxed unless they are either very new or in inordinate quantities. Nevertheless, almost anything *can* be taxed, and US customs require extremely detailed inventories of everything brought into the country – a point to remember while packing. The degree of detail legally required is ridiculous (they even like to have the titles of all books), but in practice less detail is acceptable, such as 'miscellaneous cookware and kitchen cutlery – value approximately $20'. Realistic estimated second-hand values are acceptable, but the more detailed and the more realistic your inventories are, the less trouble you are likely to have and the less likely you are to have to pay any duty. If you are seriously worried, contact the customs desk at the US Embassy: they supply an excellent information package and sample inventory list, for free, and this is well worth getting.

The last thing to consider in this chapter is how you are going to get yourself and your family out to the United States. Travelling by sea is no longer a serious option for most people: the few liners still plying the Atlantic route function more as cruise ships than as passenger carriers, and charge accordingly, while getting accommodation on cargo ships is much more difficult than you may imagine. Either way, travelling by sea will cost much more than travelling by air (even than travelling by Concorde) and so air is the realistic choice.

Air price structures are a veritable jungle, but the main options are ordinary full-price fares; excursion and advance-booking fares of various types; and special fares of various kinds, including charter fares, stand-by fares, 'bucket-shop' fares, as well as flying on super-economy airlines.

Hardly anyone pays full-price fares any more unless their companies are footing the bill; this is particularly true of full-price 'Economy' fares, which will usually entitle you to Business-class seating and an extra luggage allowance. On the other hand, these fares offer the most flexibility, as they can be bought at a moment's notice, changed, and cashed in if you do not fly; there is usually no penalty even if you do not take the flight on which you are booked, and you can change carriers almost at a whim, because the different airlines will be delighted to exchange their ticket for that of a rival.

The most familiar excursion or advance-booking fare is the APEX (Advance Passenger Excursion) fare, which must be bought at least three weeks in advance (though this period may be varied); which cannot be changed within three weeks of the outward flight date, except with very heavy penalties; which incurs smaller, but still significant penalties if the date of the return flight is changed; and which is usually only good for a maximum of a year. You can also change carriers only with difficulty, though in the event of a strike or something similar, the airline will usually do its best. One-way fares can sometimes be bought under similar conditions to APEX fares. If you know exactly when you want to travel and are unlikely to change your plans (except perhaps the return date), APEX tickets are perhaps the most useful: certainly, for short-term visits of up to one year, they represent an excellent compromise between reliability and flexibility on the one hand, and economy on the other.

Special fares are the most confusing of all. They are usually only worth investigating if you are desperate to save money, or if you are prepared to take certain (modest) risks to do so.

Charter fares are, by and large, not worth having. Your choice of destinations is limited, and you are locked into a particular schedule, which you may not be able to change at all (though holiday insurance will take care of flights missed because of circumstances genuinely beyond your control); the flights are usually on a 'cattle-truck' basis, with few amenities, with the aircraft configured to cram in as many passengers as possible, and sometimes a degree of chicanery in the seating. The authors have seen a woman on a charter flight charged full fare at the airport for her small child, though the airline had accepted a reduced fare at the time of booking, and then denied the seat which she had paid the full price for. You will certainly not be able to change carriers. In many cases, the legality of these flights is also in question, as they are supposed to cater to a pre-existing interest group who charters the aeroplane, rather than to a consortium of travel agents, and the last charter company the authors used was under investigation by the Civil Aviation Authority; we were relieved to find that they had not gone out of business by the time we returned.

Bucket-shop fares are on regular scheduled flights, and you can usually change dates, etc with little or no penalty; it is also possible, if you use a reputable bucket shop, to cash in the ticket, though there may sometimes be an administration fee. The way they work is simple: all airlines have some spare seats, and rather than fly with them empty, they sell them to bucket shops who sell them to you, the customer, at a sizeable discount – sometimes as much as half the price. The legality of the bucket shop's buying tickets and reselling them is questionable, but it is perfectly legal for you to buy them, and it is obviously in the airlines' interest to connive at the practice.

There are, however, three drawbacks to bucket-shop fares. The first is that it is virtually impossible to change carriers on the return flight, though the bucket shop will usually allow you to change carriers for the whole ticket before you go. This is no great disadvantage unless there is a strike or, worse still, your carrier goes bankrupt. In the former case, you are marooned until they choose to carry you; in the second, you are marooned, period (but remember insurance again).

The second drawback is that it is *essential* to deal with a reputable bucket shop. Some are fly-by-night operations who take a lot of money in deposits and then disappear, without ever having made a single reservation. If a place has been in the same location for some years, it is probably safe; we have never had trouble with a bucket shop going bust on us.

Thirdly, you *must* deal with a reputable airline. The very cheapest deals are usually cheap because they are very dubious set-ups – and that applies even to some of the smaller national airlines. It usually only costs a few pounds more to fly with someone you have heard of, and you can save a great deal of time, money and heartache by doing so. Not all lesser-known airlines are bad, but some are notorious, and no reputable bucket shop will recommend them, though they will sell you their tickets if you specifically request them.

All in all, bucket-shop tickets are worth while if you follow these guidelines, but you are still getting what you pay for to a certain extent. Even so, after APEX and similar fares, these are probably the tickets to go for if you want to fly children out for a visit, or something similar.

Stand-by tickets are a good buy at some times of year, when demand is low, but unless you can face the risk of hanging around an airport for two or three days in the high season, they are too high a risk for most people. You can usually change carriers, though, and the number of transatlantic carriers is such that you would usually be unlucky not to fly within twenty-four hours of arriving at the airport, though getting your luggage on the same flight is another matter. These tickets may be a good option for university-age children.

The last option, super-economy airlines, is hard to judge. Sir Freddie Laker showed the way, and his was probably the best of them; at the time of writing, his anti-trust suit against other transatlantic carriers had just been settled, and there was a hope that he might go back into the business. Since Laker, People Express and Virgin Atlantic have been offering the same sort of operation: no frills, low prices and a reliable scheduled operation. The only major drawbacks are that the prices are so low that seats are normally booked months in advance, and changing departure times at short notice is usually impossible; changing carriers is not normally possible either. For students and other low-budget travellers, these airlines are well worth considering if you can book far enough in advance, and if you do not mind the somewhat basic service, which is, however, still rather better than on most charter flights.

No matter how you buy your ticket, you can save a good deal of time and money by choosing the appropriate departure and arrival airports. In the UK, Gatwick is normally a cheaper place to fly from than Heathrow, though it is more difficult to get to unless you live in the south-east. In the United States, Boston is usually the cheapest gateway airport, and if you are hiring a car it is a more pleasant place to start from than the hurly-burly of New York. Different airlines use different gateways, too, and they often offer cheaper fares than others into their 'home' airports. If you are flying to the West, direct flights are much more convenient than changing at the East Coast, and usually cost no more, but if there are special-offer multi-sector passes available (see Chapter 2), it may prove cheaper to fly into, say, Boston or Baltimore and then change aircraft.

8

Accommodation

The cost and standard of accommodation in the United States vary enormously from place to place. Broadly, the most expensive areas are the major cities and areas of outstanding natural beauty: prices here will be comparable with the more expensive areas of central London. By contrast, the cheapest areas are out in the country, or in the suburbs of the less major cities, and here prices can be very much less than in most of Britain. Prices for the same accommodation in different parts of the country can vary by a factor of as much as ten to one.

As with any city and any country, there are also fashionable and unfashionable areas, and areas which are either on the decline or on the way up. In the Los Angeles area, for instance, Watts is definitely not a place that most people would care to live, while Inglewood has lost its nickname of 'Inglewatts' and is on the way up. By contrast, Palos Verdes is the home of the 'Yuppies' (as the joke has it, 'What do Palos Verdes wives make for dinner? – Reservations') and the super-rich live in Beverly Hills, Bel Air and Brentwood, with a beach place at Malibu. Hollywood is an 'iffy' area, good in parts but very seedy in others, but the Hollywood Hills are a much better address; Carson is increasingly a Filipino suburb. The reason for quoting all these specific examples is to show that unless you case a place very carefully, and talk to the inhabitants, you are unlikely to have the slightest chance of estimating where is a 'good' place to live, and where is not. Furthermore, the transition between a 'good' area and a 'bad' one is often very rapid. The importance of a reasonable address is not just for personal comfort and security; it also affects your credibility and social standing among other people, perhaps even more so than in Britain.

To add to the confusion, housing terms in the United States are not quite the same as they are in the UK. For example, a terraced house is a 'row home', a detached house is a 'single-family home' (the word 'home' is widely used instead of 'house'), a caravan is a 'mobile-home' or 'trailer', and what in Britain would be called a flat or maisonette is an 'apartment'; there are gradations of apartments including 'bachelor', 'studio', 'efficiency', 'walk-up' and 'cold-water', which require further explanation. Then there is the 'condominium', which is described below, and there are also local terms such as 'frame house' and 'brownstone' which are meaningless to the uninitiated.

Buying a house, as already indicated, can be an expensive business in some areas; in others, particularly where property values are rising rapidly (as in most of the Western states and Florida) it can be both economical and an excellent investment. Renting furnished or unfurnished accommodation is a good deal easier than in Britain, because tenants are not afforded the same degree of protection, and this applies whether you rent a house, an apartment or a condominium (commonly abbreviated to 'condo'). There are agencies who provide (in return for a fee) daily listings of houses, etc, for rent; they seem to do well out of it, but the usefulness of the service is not as great as it might seem. Realtors (estate agents) are generally a better bet, and so are small ads.

'Bachelor', 'studio' and 'efficiency' apartments are usually all euphemisms for single-room apartments, though not bed-sitting rooms; you will almost invariably have your own bathroom and (usually separate) kitchen. 'Cold-water' apartments are those where no hot water is supplied by the building, ie you have to have your own water-heater, and 'walk-up' is a term used mainly in New York to describe a rather seedy establishment one step up from a bed-sitting room. 'Brownstones' are in New York again, big Victorian houses which have usually been carved into cheap apartments, and a 'frame house' is a timber-built house; wood is still widely used in the United States as a building material, and wood-framed houses with wooden walls and even wooden shingles on the roof are still being built in almost all states.

A 'condo' is an apartment which shares certain facilities with other 'condos'; typically, there will be at least a swimming pool (in the West, anyway), a laundry room (a sort of laundromat dedicated to the condo block only) and a recreation room which can be used for big parties; upmarket condos may have squash and tennis courts and all kinds of facilities, even a grocery store and a beauty parlour. Because of the shared spaces, it is possible to live in rather more comfort in a condo of a given size than in a house with the same floor area (floor areas are usually quoted in advertisements for apartments and condos). Condominiums are very much the West Coast style of living, but they are appearing all over the country. They are usually bought rather than rented, with the owners running the complex as a cooperative, but you may sometimes be able to rent from an owner.

Trailers can be remarkably roomy, and are generally available as 'singlewide' or 'doublewide', corresponding to about 10ft and 20ft (3m and 6m) respectively; the overall length is normally between 40ft and 60ft (12m and 18m), so a 60ft (18m) doublewide is quite a large dwelling-place. Mobile-home parks contain between a dozen and several dozen mobile-homes, with mains services and all utilities including telephones available, and charge a modest rental. The trailers themselves can be either rented or (more usually) bought, and buying a trailer in an expensive area like Los Angeles can be an excellent investment, though you must be aware that it can be hard to get insurance for a mobile-home more than ten years old, and when a mobile-home park changes hands (which is not unusual, as they are in turn a good investment for landlords), the new landlords may require all trailers over a certain age – usually fifteen years – to be removed; certainly, they will rarely allow a trailer more than a few years old to be brought to the park. Some parks will not allow children or pets, either. It is not regarded as particularly unusual to live in a trailer, though in certain social circles it may cause raised eyebrows.

As mentioned elsewhere, standards of insulation and air-conditioning (or at least ventilation and shade) are very much higher in the United States than in the UK, but especially with older properties you should ask yourself what it would be like in high summer and in deep winter. You should also establish exactly which household appliances (if any) are included in the rental or sale contract.

A couple of factors which are unfamiliar to most British buyers are vulnerability to mud slides and earthquakes. Particularly in California, beautiful houses are slung in defiance of gravity on the sides of sheer hills, and others are built at the bottom. Come an earthquake or a heavy winter's rain, and they may all be in the middle of a thousand tons of mud at the bottom of the hill – uninsured, as no sensible insurance company will accept the risk. The same is true of insurance against brush fires, a major hazard throughout the tinder-dry summer in many places.

Whether you buy or rent, you will need to live somewhere while you are looking, and your initial exploratory vacation (see Chapter 2) is a good time to scout out temporary accommodation, and also to find somewhere to store your possessions (Chapter 7). It may of course be that accommodation is arranged for you, but even then you should have some idea of what you are getting into. In particular, you should ascertain when it will be available; exactly how much you are going to have to pay; whether or not utilities are included; whether the place is furnished or unfurnished; whether there is any particular time limit on how long you can stay in the temporary accommodation; and, of course, what sort of place it is, and whether there is enough room for the family. These points may seem obvious, but it is all too easy for an expansive, 'Oh, we'll take care of all that!' to disappear into a mass of awkward details, and it is better for that to happen *before* you arrive rather than when you stagger off the aeroplane wanting to fall into bed.

This is also the place to mention the fairly common arrangement whereby a company agrees to provide temporary accommodation for their employee while the family stays behind in the UK, the idea being that he or she will look for somewhere to live and send for them later. Although this arrangement may be superficially attractive, and indeed may be the only practicable arrangement for contract workers, it is worth remembering that you are then going to be supporting two establishments, one of which will be several thousand miles away and out of your control; that adjustment to a new country and a new job may be difficult enough without the additional strain of being separated from loved ones; that a new job is often sufficiently demanding that it leaves little time for house-hunting; that unless you like house-hunting, you may be woefully unable to find somewhere that you can be sure your spouse will like; that unless you can keep the family's momentum together, there is a risk, which grows with every week of separation, that the family may decide to stay in the UK anyway; and that there is always the risk that the partner in the US may take his or her temporary status all too literally, and fall for someone else, which may appeal to some but is normally a recipe for heartbreak on all sides.

Property taxes, similar to British rates, are assessed on the value of owned or rented property, and you will need to know how much these are and whether or not they are included in your rent. They vary from community to community, but although they are the only tax on property, they are not the only source of state and city income; there are also state sales taxes (akin to VAT) which may be supplemented further by city sales taxes, so that in Los Angeles 6 per cent of the 6.5 per cent sales tax goes to Sacramento and 0.5 per cent goes to the city, and local income taxes in addition to state taxes. These are covered further in Chapters 10 and 11.

Formerly, trailers were taxed as vehicles rather than being liable to property taxes, but the result of this was that they paid much less tax than fixed homes in return for effectively the same services, so (in California at least) the situation has changed and they now come under the Housing Department rather than the Department of Motor Vehicles; again, this is a matter of state law, and conditions elsewhere may be different.

Utilities, including electricity, water, gas (where available), telephones *and garbage collection* in some areas are billed separately, usually on a monthly basis, or sometimes every two months (it varies from place to place). If you miss a month's bill, it will be added to the next month's; miss that, and you get a warning, and eventually they will cut you off, as in Britain. Initial connections (and presumably reconnections) are usually made promptly: the telephone service, in particular, is rather quicker than in the UK. Telephone bills are itemised, call by call, which is extremely useful, but since the break-up of Ma Bell (the Bell Telephone Company), they are not always very predictable or consistent: long-distance calls inside the United States can bring some nasty surprises, including minimum-period charges instead of dialled-unit charges as in the UK. To counter this, there are various deals and special offers which your local phone company will explain to you. Utilities other than telephones may or may not be included in rentals.

All in all, it is very difficult to make generalisations about housing in the United States. In the older cities and towns of the East, you will find more European-style houses, with smaller rooms, doors to every room, and so forth, while in the West you are likely to find larger, airier rooms communicating with one another by means of archways rather than doors. As a general rule, the material standard of living of an American will be significantly higher than that of a Briton in an equivalent job in the UK, with bigger, more luxuriously and better appointed houses at almost every level. By contrast, the poor are usually poorer; but although this may have some moral impact on our readers, it is unlikely to have much practical impact.

A useful rule of thumb, already mentioned in the introduction, is to assume *regardless of the actual exchange rate* that the dollar has a purchasing power which is around half that of the pound sterling, which means that your salary will need to be at least twice as high (numerically) and that if you double the cost of your present house, you can get a fair idea of the sort of place which you might live in when you go to the United States.

Although this rule-of-thumb doubling is a very useful average, it is by no means consistent: there are some areas in which you get much better value, and others where the things which you are used to will seem prohibitively expensive. Both of these variations are spectacularly true when it comes to furnishing a house.

Consumer goods of every kind are disproportionately cheap in the United States *provided they are of domestic manufacture*, or alternatively Japanese. Thus cookers, washing machines, microwave ovens, vacuum cleaners, freezers, refrigerators and even stereo systems and so forth are all surprisingly cheap, especially if you buy in a sale: Americans are much influenced by the latest style, and last year's models will often be sold at considerable discounts. Unless you really *care* about having this year's cooker, you can save huge sums. The same is true of household furniture, but only up to a certain level of quality; beyond that, Americans tend to buy imports, and prices escalate rapidly.

As a Briton, you are effectively outside American standards of taste, and you can easily make up for having last year's washing machine (or whatever) by dotting about a few 'antiques'. In the United States, the definition of 'antique' is flexible; a cynical version is that it is anything which is old enough to fall apart, but hasn't yet. Even quite modest

British dining-room tables, for example, fetch ridiculously high prices in the United States: a good Edwardian table of no special merit is worth three to five times as much in California (which has an insatiable appetite for 'antiques'), as in its native land; and the authors have a wardrobe for which they paid £30 at auction, but which would fetch anything from $500 to $1,000 in California. Pewter plates and mugs are always a talking point, and virtually anything which is obviously European and obviously even moderately old will be venerated.

If your company is prepared to pay for shipping, it may even be worth while buying old furniture especially in the UK, as it will bring you great kudos in the US, and if you want to you can always sell it at a profit when you leave.

9
Transport

The sheer size of America means that transport is a major concern. For the purposes of this chapter, it can be divided into four categories: long-distance internal public transport, local public transport and taxis, private motoring and motorcycling, and getting about under your own steam, mainly walking and bicycling.

Air is the obvious means of internal transport, and to anyone who is used to European internal flight prices, ticket rates are likely to be a pleasant surprise. Some years ago, air travel in the United States was de-regulated, and out of the resulting free-for-all, a remarkably efficient and economical network emerged, served by a large number of carriers. In addition, there is almost always some airline, somewhere, that is offering a promotional flight to the place you want to visit. This may not be so important on business trips, where you do not want to waste your own or your secretary's time in hunting about (though a reliable and trusted travel agent will do it for you), but it may be significant if you are footing the bill. You may also wish to take advantage of 'frequent flier' programmes, in which frequent users of a particular airline are awarded bonus tickets in proportion to the distance flown; if you rack up enough business mileage in a year, you can collect a free ticket, or even two tickets, to various destinations in the United States (including Hawaii), back to Europe, or even around the world.

Something which is not immediately obvious to a European is the allocation of low, shoulder and high seasons. Basically, these follow the vacation season, which in the United States runs from Memorial Day in late May to Labor Day in early September, but there is an additional high season for internal flights (though not for most international flights) around Christmas and the New Year; there may also be a shoulder season before this, based on Thanksgiving Day in late November. The reason, of course, is that many people fly home for Thanksgiving or Christmas or both.

Amtrak has already been mentioned in Chapter 2. It is the federally administered, semi-nationalised passenger network which uses track belonging to all the old names from the songs – the Atchison, Topeka & Santa Fe, and the C&O (Chesapeake and Ohio), for example. From a business traveller's point of view, the only place where trains are taken seriously is in the north-eastern corridor, particularly from New York to Washington, though the link which goes up into Canada was being heavily promoted at the time of writing. There are also odd pockets of train-users elsewhere, such as between Los Angeles and San Diego. Otherwise, trains are only taken by those who are afraid of flying or who actually like railway trains. The Metroliner services in the north-east are reasonably fast, but there is nothing which even begins to compare with the fast European trains (including Britain's Inter-City 125). Crossing the country by train takes about three and a half *days* at best, which admittedly is a thousand miles a day, but is still a fairly unimpressive average speed (under 40mph overall). The reason for this sloth is mainly poor maintenance of the permanent way, but there is also a tradition of very long, very slow trains throughout the country. As a matter of interest, American railway lines are rarely fenced off, and automatic-barrier crossings are not common; the tracks still run through towns as they used to in Western movies, and the trains rely on their whistles and lights to warn people to get off the line, which perhaps gives some indication of how slow they are and of how long you have to wait if a train is crossing the road.

Long-distance buses have also been mentioned in Chapter 2, but it is worth reiterating here that despite (or perhaps because of) their comparatively low fares, they are not a very attractive proposition. Not only are the bus stations usually in the least attractive part of town, but the gigantic distances involved in travelling in the Midwest, or going across the country, mean that you have to be very hardy indeed to try a long journey, while for shorter journeys you might as well drive. Nevertheless, for the hardy, they are a good way to see America, and you may care to entrust your teenage children to them. They also provide an excellent low-cost means of hauling even quite large pieces of luggage about the country, accompanied or unaccompanied; some friends of the authors sent a large trunk from San Francisco to Los Angeles for about a third of the price of the nearest competitive means of transport.

Local public transport in most of the United States is, quite frankly, of a very poor standard. It is probably at its most efficient in New York, where the (rather confusing) underground railway serves most of Manhattan Island very well, and many of the surrounding suburbs adequately. Unfortunately, it is filthy and dangerous: there are signs in the stations urging passengers to stay in the central cars at night, and some idea of New Yorkers' attitudes can be gained from the favourable publicity which surrounded a man who shot and killed or seriously injured three youths who tried to mug him: he was a popular hero. As for the much-publicised graffiti, there is precious little art in it; most of it is illiterate vandalism. The subway authority itself is a dab hand at vandalism, too: many of the beautiful old stations have suffered as much from casually made additions and alterations, where holes knocked in the walls and ceilings have not even been plastered over, as from the spray-can brigade.

The other city where public transport is strong is San Francisco, where the Bay Area Rapid Transit System (BART) provides an adequate, though not comprehensive, underground railway system, and the cable cars (refurbished in the early-to-mid 1980s) provide a very good and rather entertaining means of public transport, albeit at a price, as well as a tourist attraction.

Apart from this, although there are buses in most major and minor cities, they do not run very often or very predictably, and they are used mostly by the poor or by children who are not old enough to drive, so the local transit authority never worries very much about the quality of the service. Coverage is poor, and speeds through the crowded city streets are low. Besides, bus routes are always much harder to learn than train routes, because they do not lend themselves readily to schematics and controlled passengerflow, let alone easy interchanges, so you need to be either dedicated or needy to learn enough to get about on a bus. A possible exception is shuttle minibuses, which run over particularly well-travelled routes in some city centres, and can save a useful few minutes' walking time. Schoolchildren are normally transported in special yellow-painted school buses, rather than using regular public buses; these have fixed pick-up points all over the city, and in the country too. There is no charge for public school buses in most places. It is usually compulsory for all traffic to stop when a school bus is stopped to pick up or discharge children: flashing lights on the bus itself warn of this.

Park-and-ride out-of-town car parks are operated in many cities, though they are not always widely used; for short visits, they are not even particularly economical or time-saving, as parking in almost all American cities (except perhaps New York) is vastly easier than in central London; even in downtown Washington DC, you can easily find a parking meter within a few minutes.

Taxis are more widely used in the compact cities of the East than in the expansive West, where the distances involved make costs prohibitive. Once again, New York City is something of an oddity: it is often quicker to walk if you are only travelling ten or even twenty blocks, because of the traffic, but a taxi does save you from arriving at your destination looking all hot and bothered. In most places the 'rule of two' rule of thumb applies: a taxi ride costs about twice as much in dollars as you would expect it to be in pounds. Taxis are all metered, but it is worth remembering that the driver may be unable to change large-denomination bills.

As already indicated in the second chapter, you will need a motor-car if you are in the United States for anything but the briefest vacation, and have any intention of leaving the place where you are staying. Your entire perspective on motoring changes: with big wide roads, parking lots everywhere (except perhaps in the oldest parts of the oldest Eastern towns) and cheap gasoline, motoring is very much easier than anywhere in Europe. A small car, ideal for burrowing through London or Paris, begins to look ridiculous; a typical British medium-sized Ford or Austin looks tiny; even a good-sized car, a Jaguar or a Rover, is classified as a 'compact'. We shall return to this later.

You can drive for up to a year on your British licence in most states, though if you are staying in one state for more than a year, local state law may require you to take a state test sooner – within six or even three months – because you have shown the intention of moving to the state in question. Some states also require you to surrender all other driving licences, or at least those from other states, though rather than go through the inconvenience of trying to extract a duplicate from the DVLC in Swansea, it is perhaps easiest to deny that you have any other licences, or to say that you have lost them. Most people, such as car-hire agencies and even the police, prefer a British licence to an International Driving Permit for some reason; the authors have proffered an IDP and been asked for a 'real' licence.

Because American driving licences are a matter of state law, rather than federal, the rules and regulations vary widely. The age at which you can get a licence (commonly called a *driver's*, rather than a *driving*, licence) also varies, and there are ramifications undreamt of in Britain, such as (in some states) a permit for sixteen-year-olds which allows you to drive until dark on your own, but requires you to have a qualified driver with you after dark until you are eighteen. L-plates are little used, except by professional driving schools, but many high schools teach driving as a part of the curriculum: anyone who cannot (or will not) drive before they are out of their teens is regarded as something of a curiosity.

The tests themselves also vary widely, but the test for driving a car in most states is more rigorous in form, though easier to pass, than in the UK. It is quite usual for there to be a parking-lot 'slalom' test with cones, a written test on the state highway code, and a formal eyesight test (possibly including depth-perception tests), as well as an on-the-road test in the British manner. On the other hand, the slalom test is undemanding (unless perhaps you are driving an old-fashioned twenty-foot gas guzzler), and the on-the-road test is scarcely more difficult.

Licences are valid for varying periods, and the procedure for renewal is again different from state to state: in some it is automatic, in others the eyesight and written tests are taken again, and if you are over retirement age it is theoretically possible in some states that you may be required to re-take the whole test periodically. The delay in getting a test is very much less than in the UK, usually twenty-four hours at most, and the fee is also much lower, only a few dollars. As the State of California puts it in the material which they hand out to driving-test candidates, when you consider the number of people that pass every year, there is really nothing to worry about . . .

Which is exactly what there is to worry about. The average American driver is vastly less competent than the average

British driver, precisely because driving is so much less demanding. Many drivers are reasonably competent in slow-moving traffic, but as soon as the traffic flow begins to speed up, they begin to get quite frightening. This is bad enough on an uncrowded road in town, but on the freeways, most people drive far too close to the car in front (even more so than in the UK), and something which is terrifying to a British driver with rigid ideas about lane discipline is that there is no law against overtaking on the near side. Those vast Californian freeways, with five lanes going in each direction, may be somewhat faster in the extreme left lane than in the extreme right, but someone who is in a real hurry will carve from one lane to another with abandon — and, indeed, repeated lane-switching for overtaking will get you a traffic citation in California much faster than exceeding the speed limit. If you are rolling along in the left most lane at 65mph, you are unlikely to get a ticket, and if someone is travelling at 50mph in the leftmost lane and you overtake him at 55mph (or even 60mph) on the nearside, you are unlikely to get a ticket; but if you are determined to go quickly through the usual wandering, wavering morass of drivers who sprawl across all five lanes, you are very likely indeed to be cited (if you don't kill yourself first). In a hundred miles of multi-lane California freeway, on a clear bright morning with no visible dangers, the authors once saw five multiple-vehicle accidents, though apparently without any serious injuries. Drivers of pick-up trucks are the worst offenders — we accurately predicted two of those five accidents on the basis of appalling driving by pick-up truck drivers, and came upon them a few miles later — but big trucks are tremendous bullies, and will drive within a few feet of your tail in the hope of intimidating you into moving over (they are not allowed into the fastest lanes on highways with three or more lanes). In the authors' experience, Chicago is one of the worst places in the world to drive — it makes Hyde Park Corner, or the Etoile in Paris, seem like a drive in the country.

If there are any enthusiastic motorcyclists among our readers, the news is almost all bad. American motorcycle driving tests are mostly perfunctory — when the riders bother to take them at all — and in many states there are no restrictions about the size of motorcycle which a raw novice may ride upon the road, so a sixteen-year-old who is rich enough may buy a 140mph Japanese superbike and enjoy a riding career which is meteoric in both its speed and its duration. Most motorcyclists are totally incompetent, which does nothing for the reputation of motorcycling generally, and motorists are vastly more hostile to motorcyclists than in the UK; deliberate attempts to unseat and kill motorcyclists are reported every month in the American motorcycling press. In the East, Puritanism encourages the police to be very hard on motorcyclists, and across most of the rest of the country the sheer tedium of trundling along on wide flat roads at absurdly low speeds accounts for the popularity of the horrid 'full-dress tourer', a monstrous motorcycle which can weigh over 900lb (400kg) *unladen*, and may then be used to tow a trailer (for non-motorcycling readers, a British police BMW weighs about 500lb/225kg). Only in California is motorcycling a real pleasure for many people, and even there, real addicts have to look hard for twisting roads on which to exercise any riding skill.

Whether you ride or drive, insurance is now compulsory in most states, but it is not always taken very seriously: the percentage of uninsured drivers in the US is much greater than in the UK, and, it must be said, the insurance companies are more willing to avoid meeting legitimate claims whenever possible. As an example, a major American insurance company tried to avoid liability for a $1,500 claim made by one of the authors on the grounds of a $3 discrepancy in the payment of a $750 premium, a discrepancy of which they had made no previous mention, and which arose because of a simple arithmetical error in a complex interchange of rebate and re-insurance when she moved from a low-risk insurance area to a higher one. A threat of legal action soon brought them to heel, but this does provide a useful insight into American business ethics, on which there will be more in Chapter 11.

As may be seen from the size of that premium, which was for a woman in her thirties with a clean driving record in the late 1970s, insurance in many parts of the United States is very expensive indeed – although she did carry full third-party liability, passenger liability, own-damage liability and uninsured-driver liability (against being hit by uninsured drivers, which was in fact what happened when she was stopped at an intersection). It is also worth noting that the third-party personal-injury risk carried by the insurer in many states is *not* unlimited, as it is by law in the UK, and that the minimum legal limit may be, for example, $100,000, a derisory figure when compared with potential million-dollar suits. The authors are fervent believers in insurance, and believe that it is well worth taking as much insurance as possible. Finally, in many states the penalties for driving without insurance are laughably low: in California, until 1985, there was *no* penalty for being uninsured as long as you did not have an accident, and when penalties were introduced, the *maximum* fine was $100! Compare this with the size of premiums, and it is small wonder that the improvident (and the worst drivers) are often uninsured. For comprehensive insurance in the US, a person with a clean driving record can expect to pay three or four times as much (after allowance for currency conversion) in the US as in the UK, comparing like with like (central New York, Chicago or LA with central London; rural Kansas with Devon).

Apart from the generally low standard of driving, other matters which are of particular note are speed limits; parking; the frequency of stops in cities; the freedom to turn on a red light; compulsory-turn lanes; and the standards of roads.

As already intimated, the 'double nickel' 55mph speed limit is not taken seriously; some measure of its disrepute may be gained from the fact that in the mid-1980s, the federal government threatened to withhold federal highway funding from any state unless *at least 50 per cent* of the motorists in that state could be shown to observe the speed limit (buried induction loops in the road were used for testing). A law so poorly observed could hardly but bring the law in general into disrepute, though some states enforce it more enthusiastically than others – which effectively means more arbitrarily and unpredictably, because it is impossible to enforce uniformly and consistently. The best thing to do is to stay within the 55mph limit until you get a feeling for the de facto speed limit and the attitudes of the police in a particular state, and then speed up accordingly.

Inside towns, speed limits are more widely observed, though on most main streets they are a realistic 35mph or 40mph. Near schools, the limit may drop to 25mph or even 15mph, though this is usually only applicable when children are present (in which case it will say so), and in well-to-do suburbs the limit may also be 25mph. These lower speeds are seldom strictly observed, and as in the UK two or three miles an hour over the higher limits is seldom cause for a ticket unless you are obviously driving unsafely. A special note on New England states is that they often post speed limits which are unrealistically low even on the open road (50mph is common), and that on winding roads they will post official speed limits on the corners. In the West, and indeed in most of the rest of the country, such corner limits are advisory (on yellow backgrounds rather than white), but in New England they are compulsory. You will soon learn how realistic these corner limits are in different states, and for different cars: in a Jaguar, the authors found that a 50mph or 55mph corner could safely be taken at any speed (provided there was sufficient visibility); that corners labelled from 25mph to 45mph could safely be taken 10mph faster; and that for anything slower (such as might appear on the Pacific Coast Highway, or in the Rockies), one could rarely safely take it at more than 5mph over the stated speed.

Free parking is usually provided by most modern stores, and there is usually plenty (at least by British standards) of on-street metered or even free parking. It is illegal to park against the flow of the traffic: in other words, you must park on the nearside, except in one-way streets. Meter periods usually run from fifteen minutes (outside banks and the like) to three or four hours, and are much cheaper than in Britain, and meters may be 'fed' additional money when the initial period expires. Otherwise, downtown parking lots are inclined to be expensive, though you may be able to get a reduction or a period of free parking via 'validation', which means presenting a bill from a neighbourhood store which you have visited while parked there.

Inside towns and cities, Americans are great believers in traffic lights and four-way stops, which are an infuriating delay to those brought up on the concept of minor roads yielding priority to major ones. Traffic lights introduce no great difficulties, except for two differences. First, they are frequently set on the *far* side of an intersection, which can make judging where to stop difficult, and secondly, you can turn right against a red light in most states (possibly all by the time you read this – the practice originated in California but rapidly spread through the country). You must stop at the light, as though it were a stop sign, but if the way is clear you can then continue on your way unless there is a sign expressly forbidding you to do so (it usually says 'NO TURN ON RED').

Four-way stops, on the other hand, are a poisonous invention whereby *all* traffic must stop at a crossroads, and then proceed in the order in which they arrived at the stop: in the case of simultaneous arrival, the car on your right has right of way. Four-way stops are made all the more irritating by three factors. First, a dead stop is essential: a rolling stop, where the car slows to almost nothing but does not actually stop dead, can get you a ticket. Secondly, the placing of stop signs is frequently fairly arbitrary, there may not be a limit line on the road, and the sign itself may be obscured by vegetation. Thirdly, in addition to two-way stops (where traffic on one road has priority and need not stop), you will sometimes find a three-way stop, where traffic from one direction at a crossroads has priority but the other three directions have to stop. It is not always easy to tell what sort of junction is which, so extreme care is necessary and you must be prepared for those who do know the junction (or are simply in a hurry) to blare their horns and shout at you.

Compulsory-turn lanes are exactly what their name implies. They are usually signalled by 'Right Lane MUST Turn Right' or 'left Lane MUST Turn Left', and if you leave it too late before getting out of one of these lanes, you lay yourself open to a ticket, abuse from fellow drivers, and possibly being rammed. To make life more interesting, although most freeways have right-hand exits, there are sometimes left-hand exits too.

Finally, road standards vary enormously. Interstate highways are mostly of UK motorway standard or better, usually with vast central reservations, though some in Illinois in particular are reminiscent of the worst-maintained German *autobahns*. At the other extreme, especially in the Western states, there are many roads which are of oil-bound gravel, plain gravel, or just dirt, though these are usually *very* secondary. In between, most roads are better surfaced and better maintained than most in Europe, though those of some cities are of an extremely poor standard: New York in particular is a mass of potholes, called 'chuckholes' in the US. Most roads have broad shoulders, but in the country the drop-off between the road surface and the dirt shoulder can be considerable, and can give the suspension quite a pounding. Really roughly surfaced car parks are not unusual in the country, and in the city there are often high humps and bumps on entering or leaving car parks, as well as awkward dips for drainage when crossing some streets, and railway lines which run along humps in the middle of the street (or across it). Cars with limited ground clearance can wipe off exhaust pipes and other low-lying accessories, and vehicles with a large overhang over the wheels can crunch and ground their extremities.

In winter, snow-chains or studded tyres may be required by law on many roads, though four-wheel-drive vehicles with appropriate 'all weather' tyres are often an acceptable substitute. This requirement is no empty bureaucracy, as you will find if you try to drive without them.

For most people, it is not worth importing their own vehicles, even temporarily. Although temporary importation does not necessarily obligate the vehicle owner to meet increasingly strict federal emission regulations (which are even more strict in California), many cars will suffer from terrible indigestion as a result of low-octane American petrol, which is typically 88 for 'regular' and 93 for 'premium'; for comparison, British two-star is normally 91–2 octane, three-star is 93–5 octane, and four-star is 96–8 octane. What is worse, 'premium' is typically 30–40 per cent more expensive than 'regular'. If you have a classic car which can run (or can be made to run) on very low octane fuel, and if it is pre-1966, you can import it with impunity; about the only emission modification required will be the addition of a crankcase breather draining into the sump, and on pre-1956 cars there are no requirements at all (though check this carefully, because regulations can change). Transporting a vehicle across the Atlantic may cost less than you expect, but it is still a stiff expense: the two-way trip would cost about the same as a couple of months' car hire, and then you would need to consider the dockside charges at both ends, the time and bureaucracy involved, and the insurance.

'Federalising' a post-1966 car to meet appropriate emission requirements cost at the time of writing anything from about $1,000 to about $12,000, depending on the car and the year; customs officials can tell many sad stories of cars being destroyed because they could not be made to meet federal or Californian emission standards, or because a similar model had never been crash-tested à la Ralph Nader. Even if you import an American-specification car privately, gasoline-powered cars are likely to require considerable work – at least the installation of a new catalytic converter – because they have already been run on leaded gas. Unleaded gas is required for all modern cars imported into the United States, and it is a federal offence to introduce leaded gas into the tank of a vehicle marked 'Unleaded Fuel Only', but unleaded gas is not readily available in most of Europe. Diesels may be a better bet, but even then you are going to have plenty of bureaucracy to contend with.

It must be said, though, that it may be worth importing a new car when the dollar is strong: in early 1985, some Mercedes-Benz models were as much as $20,000 cheaper in Germany than in the US, and even after you had paid for transport and federalising, you were still more than $10,000 to the good. Against this, unless you have imported the car through the manufacturer's own European-delivery service (some do operate one, though savings are less marked than for a do-it-yourself operation) you have no warranty and you may meet with downright hostility from some dealers when you try to get work done. All in all, it is not a good option. With motorcycles, the position is slightly different, and if you want to import, say, a Hesketh or a Laverda, you may find life easier. There is, however, a surcharge imposed on motor-cycles of over 700cc as a protectionist measure to help Harley-Davidson.

Car hire has already been covered in Chapter 2, and need not concern us again, which only leaves buying a car inside the US. Whether you are buying new or used, there is a good deal to be said for buying an American car, because you will get a lot of car for your money and spares will be reasonably readily available. Alternatively, increasing numbers of Americans are buying Japanese cars, which handle vastly better than most American cars and are usually much more economical to run. If you can afford it, though, it is well worth buying a British car. It will be good for your image – there is tremendous prestige associated with all imported cars, except perhaps Japanese – and most Americans are patriotic, and will take your purchase of a British car as saying the same about you. The authors have driven Jaguars extensively in the United States, and can confirm from personal experience that they attract a good deal of attention, all of it favourable, as well as being superb cars for American roads. They are comfortable and luxurious when cruising along interstate highways, fast enough and smooth-braking enough to drive out of the way of dangerous drivers, and, of course, very powerful and sweet-handling when you do get a chance to drive on a twisty road. The fuel consumption, which may seem alarming in Britain, becomes trivial with American gas prices, and in any case low speeds and emission-controlled engines can lead to surprising economy: we recorded an average of 15–16mpg for an XJ-S, and up 21mpg for an XJ6. These are miles per *American* gallon, too: in imperial measure, they translate into close to 20mpg for the XJ-S, and 25mpg for the XJ6.

Compared with European cars, most American models seem festooned with unnecessary gewgaws and ornamentation, but there are two accessories which are little considered in the UK but almost essential in the US: these are air-conditioning and cruise control. Air-conditioning is merely a convenience in England, where temperatures rarely climb out of the 80s Fahrenheit (27–32°C) but in New York City on a muggy 90°F (32°C) day, or in the desert at 110°F (44°C), they are virtually a necessity. There is a fuel-consumption penalty of about 1mpg when using the air-conditioner, which is another argument for a powerful car: in a Ford Tempo the authors once drove, the car slowed detectably when the air-conditioner compressor cut in! It is also important to have a large, efficient and clean radiator when you are using the air-conditioner in the mountains: sometimes, there are warnings posted to switch off the air-conditioner when ascending a long grade, in order to avoid overheating. Many American cars will boil, but a deliberate attempt to provoke the Jaguars into overheating barely stirred the temperature gauge needle from the 'normal' mark.

The cruise control is still sufficiently rare in the UK to be worth explaining. Basically, you press a button when you are travelling at the speed you want, and the car will hold that speed up hill and down dale. You can accelerate beyond that speed for passing, and a touch on the brake or changing into a lower gear will cancel it, after which you can resume it with a touch of the 'resume' switch once you are in top again. It has two enormous advantages in the United States. First, it makes holding a chosen speed easy, whereas you may otherwise find your velocity creeping up or down as you drive along the endless freeways, inviting delay on the one hand or a speeding ticket on the other. This alone makes driving long distances much less tiring. Secondly, it can do wonders for your fuel consumption, improving it by as much as 10–15 per cent on a long run by keeping the engine running at precisely the throttle setting required, and no more.

Even quite small cars are often equipped with cruise control in the United States, though the bigger the engine, the less effect you feel when ascending or descending hills. For example, the 5.3 litre V12 in the Jaguar XJ-S was completely indifferent to hills, while the 4.2 litre straight-six will slow to 45mph on long, straight mountain grades if you do not lose your patience first and drop down into a lower gear (where it will do 70mph again). Smaller engines still tend to give up completely even on comparatively minor hills, until you *have* to change gear. Nevertheless, a 2 litre Honda which the authors also drove still proved the worth of the cruise control on the long straight roads of the Arizona and California deserts.

If you decide to buy a used car, it is worth remembering that very few Americans look after their cars (or any other sort of machinery) at all carefully, and that the mechanical condition of even an externally well-cared-for car may be very poor indeed. Unless you are a mechanical expert, an independent assessment of the condition and price of a car may be well worth while, and remember that American used-car warranties are often very short and substantially worthless anyway: thirty days is usual, and ninety days is exceptional, even for quite high-priced cars from reputable dealers, and there is nothing like as much consumer-protection legislation in most American states as there is in the UK. If at all possible, it is best to buy in the Sunbelt, because there is no snow there in the winter, and therefore no salt on the roads, and therefore far less corrosion: a Californian car can be free from significant rust after twenty years or more.

It is also important to look very carefully indeed at second-hand imported cars, and to check the spares position. Some (such as Jaguar again, or Porsche, or BMW) may be very good; others may no longer be imported, and you can be in serious trouble. It is also worth noting that while there may be plenty of dealers in, say, southern California, the position in Kansas, where *any* import is a rarity, may be very

Yes, Virginia, cops *do* still ride Harley-Davidson motorcycles, carry guns, swing their truncheons, and call you 'Mac'. This one is in Washington DC. American cops generally are less helpful than British ones, but they find it hard to resist a British accent and 'Excuse me, officer . . .'

Every state has its own central government building or 'Capitol'; this is
California's State Capitol in Sacramento

different. Paradoxically, British 'classics' such as the Big Healeys and the old TR-series sports cars can often be bought very cheaply in the US, particularly in California where their bodywork will almost invariably be better than in the UK, but trying to find the parts to repair them or a mechanic who can work on them, at least at an affordable price, will not be easy.

For a really cheap car, a big old gas guzzler such as a Cadillac or a Chrysler New Yorker can be a good buy, because the massive low-stressed V-8 motors and drive trains last for ever, though ancillaries such as the electric windows and seat adjustments may die off over the decades, and the handling may well frighten you silly. There is also the fuel consumption to consider: it can drop as low as 8mpg around town, and is unlikely to exceed 15mpg even on a long run.

Finally, we come to the question of moving under your own steam in the United States. In New York particularly, roller-skates and skateboards seem to be regarded as a normal mode of transport, and you see intrepid individuals scooting among the traffic. Most of our readers, though, will be more concerned with walking, though a few may wish to ride bicycles.

Contrary to popular reports, it is unusual for a pedestrian to be stopped for questioning just because he or she is a pedestrian, even in Los Angeles. People *do* walk from A to B, especially downtown, and in central New York and San Francisco, for example, it is perfectly feasible to walk everywhere. On the other hand, most people will drive from one store to another, partly because crossing American streets can be a traumatic experience and partly because there is not the desperate need to find a parking place and to cling to it. As already mentioned, you can be given a ticket for crossing other than at a traffic light or other authorised place, and American drivers generally do not expect to see, or to make any allowance for, pedestrians crossing elsewhere. Even the ill-marked legal crosswalks (marked in different ways in every state, and almost in every city) are not particularly safe: you certainly do not have the automatic right of way that you do on a British zebra crossing, though those who have tried to cross a road in Paris will be familiar with the motorists' attitude.

Cycling is generally seen more as a means of exercise than as a means of getting from one place to another, and there are a number of excellent cycle tracks in improbable and very attractive locations, such as alongside many beaches in Los Angeles or high in the Rocky Mountains in Colorado. Cycle touring is also growing in popularity, and the run down the Pacific Coast Highway is a classic. Otherwise, cycling on city streets (or indeed anywhere else) is risky, and is not improved by the extraordinary American custom of cycling in the road *in the direction of oncoming traffic*. There seem to be no very clear rules on this terrifyingly dangerous practice, and in some states most cyclists will ride with the traffic while in others almost all will ride against it. Motorists are even less considerate of cyclists than they are of motorcyclists, and deliberate harassment is by no means unusual, so with the exception of the more remote towns and (once again) New York City, few adults ride bicycles.

If you are prepared to let your children ride, or if you want to ride for exercise, buy European bicycles. American 'sports' bikes are impossibly heavy, typically weighing twice as much as a British, French or Italian machine, and they are not much fun to ride. They can, however, support two children: an alarmingly common sight in American suburbs is a good-sized teenage boy riding his bicycle with his teenage girlfriend balanced on the handlebars, wobbling all over the wrong side of the road. Some idea of the loathing with which motorcyclists are regarded is that many parents, in one survey, said that they would rather have their daughters carried like this than on a motorcycle pillion!

10
Shopping and Services

Shopping in the US can be very different from shopping in the UK. Both brand names and the kinds of goods available are often different, though you also may find familiar products under different brand names, or familiar brand names on unfamiliar products. One of the most important differences lies in the kinds of shops which most people patronise. Rather than going to small individual shops, they go to department stores, supermarkets and 'malls'. Furthermore, instead of going 'in town' to shop, most people in big cities go to neighbourhood suburban shopping developments, which usually keep longer hours than city-centre stores and often offer a wider choice of all but the most specialised merchandise.

Department stores developed to a very high degree in the US, and in the fifties and sixties usually provided the best service and the lowest prices available. As in the UK, centralised purchasing brought the best possible prices, but service was stressed and the sales staff were expected to give each customer individual attention. In the seventies, the discount store started to appear, also buying in volume, but cutting sales staff to the bare minimum and undercutting the department stores until they too had to cut sales staff or lose the competitive edge. Today, the department stores still offer better value than the small stores can, but the service is not what it was; this, combined with the popularity of malls (see below) has led to something of a resurgence of more specialised stores.

Supermarkets are very similar to their British counterparts, but are usually much larger (more like a British hypermarket) and stock a much wider variety of merchandise. Rather than going to a separate baker, butcher, grocer and greengrocer, most Americans prefer the convenience of one-stop shopping; and unlike the UK, where the individual stores are often cheaper than the supermarket and offer a better choice, in the US, the supermarkets have the edge. This is because centralised purchasing is very much better organised than in the UK, and the large grocery chains go in turn to large distribution chains; there are not the fragmented markets, jobbers, wholesalers and so forth that are found in Britain.

It is sometimes hard to draw a clear distinction between a department store and a supermarket, because many supermarkets sell not only consumables – food, drink, stationery, batteries and the like – but also various kinds of durables. At the least, they are likely to sell ice-chests (the insulated boxes for keeping ice used to keep food and drink cold on picnics, etc), small electrical goods and parts, and photographic films, and they may well also sell cameras and radios, and even guns and ammunition.

Adjusting to shopping for food in supermarkets can be difficult if you are used to using traditional small shops, but you can make life easier (and save money) by planning ahead and using coupons. These are used to a vastly greater extent than in the UK, and most local newspapers run a weekly food section with advertisements (often full-page or multi-page) placed by major supermarkets. These advertisements incorporate both merchandise and store coupons, which offer cash discounts, 'two-for-one' deals, and other incentives. These are usually well worth clipping: some stores even offer 'double coupons', which allow you to obtain *double* the discount offered by merchandise coupons. 'Merchandise' coupons are provided by the manufacturer of a given item, and are generally honoured by any merchant, while the 'store' coupons will be usable only in a particular store. Some stores will, however, honour coupons from other stores to prevent their regular customers being tempted away, or if they feel their business needs a boost. This is especially true of double coupons: for example, even major chains like Safeway will sometimes advertise that they will honour any other stores' double coupons. Although this may all sound like more trouble than it is worth, you can regularly save between 10 per cent and 15 per cent of your weekly grocery bill by using the food section, clipping the coupons, and planning your shopping carefully. Many Americans carry wallet-like folders with the coupons organised by category; you can buy these, or they are often given away as promotional items. It is as well to check through the coupons in the 'coupon organiser' from time to time, as they may carry an expiry date.

The shopping mall, a larger, more sophisticated version of the British shopping centre, has become commonplace throughout the US. They feature almost every kind of shop under one roof, from small specialty shops (in Los Angeles there is one specialising entirely in silly hats!) to bookshops, health-food shops, delicatessens, shoe shops and even supermarkets and department stores. There are multi-screen movie theatres, and all sorts of restaurants, from stand-up fast food to sit-down-and-order places, and most kinds of food are available, from health food to ethnic specialities. There is usually at least one bank, a hairdresser and an optician, and in some of the biggest, newest malls there are car-rental offices, airline reservation counters, and even art galleries. Muzak plays in the background, there are machines and arcades to keep the children amused, and malls are increasingly the meeting place and recreation hall for teenagers − 'Mallies' or 'Mall brats'. Malls began in the Eastern US where the weather made going from place to place inconvenient and uncomfortable; at first they were just small shopping centres, usually with only an awning-like roof between the stores, but as they grew and became more widely accepted they were enclosed completely. Some people, though, find them oppressive: the crowds, and the constant background noise of Muzak, children playing, babies crying and so forth create an environment reminiscent of Christmas Eve panic shopping, every day of the year.

Increasingly, all specialty shops are to be found in malls; old downtown areas are torn down, and rather than replacing them with the same sort of buildings, shopping malls and office blocks are built instead; some malls actually form the lower floors of multi-storey office blocks. Exceptions to this general rule are in the East, where buildings tend to be left up longer, and commercial (as distinct from consumer) stores of all kinds still inhabit the older premises: thus, a domestic computer shop or stationers might be in a mall, but a commercial or business supplier would more likely be in an old-fashioned individual shop.

Opening hours vary widely. In the big cities, many (but not all) suburban supermarkets are open twenty-four hours a day, seven days a week. Suburban department stores are usually open from 9am to 9pm, though specialty stores in malls may close earlier (the whole mall will usually be closed at 10pm or 11pm), while city-centre stores may close as early as 6pm. Although Sunday opening is the rule, hours are often shorter on a Sunday, and in some states, particularly in the Midwest, there are still 'blue' laws which restrict opening hours, so that the hours and days of opening are very like the traditional British ones. 'Blue' laws may also affect the opening hours of liquor stores; in some states, markets which sell liquor (as distinct from liquor stores) may be open to sell other goods, but banned from selling liquor at particular hours.

Liquor is a special case in many ways. Identification (ID) is usually demanded if the shopkeeper even begins to suspect that you are under age, and liquor stores are subject to many more restrictions than most others. In Colorado, for example, a liquor store is not allowed to sell peanuts and crisps, because that constitutes 'incitement to drink' in a way that merely selling alcohol does not. Colorado bars, on the other hand, are obliged to provide snacks to help soak up the alcohol . . .

The minimum legal drinking age varies from state to state; it is further confused by the way that many states have two different drinking ages, one for weak 'three-two' beer (which includes most domestic products) and one for stronger beers, wines, and spirits. There has been a move lately to *increase* the drinking age in many states, and more and more now allow you to drink 'three-two' beer at 19, and real beer, wines, and spirits only at 21!

One last type of specialised store is the 'drugstore', which is essentially a glorified chemist's shop, but which also sells all kinds of other things, including perhaps food, liquor, stationery, hardware and even clothes: Boots the Chemists, in the UK, are very similar to an American drugstore. The drugstore soda fountain, that staple of American movies and fiction in the 1950s and before, is now very rare, but it can still sometimes be found, especially in 'Olde Towne' tourist areas.

So much for the stores themselves; what about the goods they sell? We have already touched upon this to a certain extent, but it is worth looking at a few specific areas to see what is available: clothing, food and consumer durables will show some of the differences and similarities.

Whether you buy in a department store or a specialty shop,

buying clothes in the US differs very little from in the UK, except that (as already mentioned) department stores usually have the best value for money. The disadvantages to buying in a department store, particularly in a small community, is that a lot of your friends may turn up dressed identically! Small stores, or mail order (see below), are the answer to this, unless you are habitually dressed by Pierre Cardin, Balenciaga or Kenzo.

Although the goods may be similar, both pricing and sizing can be something of a surprise. Most basics, such as underpants, jeans, T-shirts and so forth are generally cheaper in the US, particularly after you have made allowance for the generally higher salaries, but some unexpected items cost more: bras are an example. Sizing is only confusing if you read the meaningless descriptions such as (for girls' clothes) 'pre-teens', 'sub-teens' 'missey's', 'junior', and so forth, but American women's sizes are *not* the same as UK sizes. If you wear a 12 in the UK, you will need a 10 in the US; a 10 will be an 8; and so on. The exact opposite is true of shoes, for both men and women: a British 4 will be an American 5 or even 5½, a British 7 an American 8 or 8½, and so on.

In any case, buying shoes brings its own problems. Firstly, most shoe stores adopt the Procrustean approach of catering only to those with an average-width foot. Secondly, women's leather shoes are becoming increasingly hard to find, partly because the shoe industry has become a fashion industry and shoes must be cheap enough to be replaced each season, and partly due to pressure from conservation groups who feel it is immoral to wear leather. Men's leather shoes are much easier to find, but the same process is detectably beginning there too – and besides, American men's shoes are usually of much worse quality than British. The solutions here are either mail-order again, or buying imported shoes, which is not easy in the face of American protectionism. Alternatively, you can get the most magnificent cowboy-style boots, in innumerable styles from comparatively conservative to downright vivid (such as purple lizard with ostrich-skin inlays). There are whole stores devoted to nothing but boots, not even selling shoes. If you don't wear boots, buy your shoes in Britain or elsewhere in Europe.

On the subject of dress generally, most people throughout the US tend to be very conservative by European standards.

Even where clothes are casual, they are conservatively casual (jeans, open-necked shirts, etc) instead of the very individualistic styles so often seen in the UK. This is true even of the young: punks (called 'punkers' in some parts of the US) were a rarity even in New York and Los Angeles when they were an everyday sight in Britain. After a while, the sight of a teenager with fluorescent pink hair and a jewel in the nose is a welcome relief from the waves of conformity! Perhaps the only *really* European-style city in that respect is San Francisco, where (presumably) the hippies' children love to dress to shock their parents. On the East Coast, as mentioned elsewhere, people tend both to 'dress up' and to dress more formally than in the West; while you may see plenty of women in skirts and men in sports jackets back East, jeans and casual clothes are more common out West.

A very good indicator of typical everyday fashion in the US is the mail-order catalogue. Unlike the UK, where mail-order caters mainly to the bottom end of the market and costs more than going to the shop, American catalogues often offer better value for money than retail outlets, and a wider variety of merchandise, ranging from the frankly tacky to the offerings of high-quality specialty houses. Some catalogues are associated with major retail chains – Sears/Sears Roebuck is the best-known example, with over 200,000 items in their catalogue, from ladies' underwear to motorcycles and chain saws – and the catalogue order may often be placed at the retail outlet and picked up there the next day. The big mail-order houses never have agents, but deal directly with the customer. It is fairly safe to send for items from almost any mail-order company, as the federal consumer-protection laws governing the sale of goods through the mail are far more strict than most consumer-protection laws in the US, which are usually a state matter. A significant difference between US and UK catalogues is that while payment in the UK is usually 'on the never', a small sum a week, you pay cash or use your charge card when buying from an American catalogue.

In addition to the big companies like Sears, there are many small mail-order companies. Some specialise in tools, some in 'sporting goods' (ie guns), some in work clothes and footwear, some in needlework and crafts, and there are many good seasonal catalogues, especially at Christmas; Bachman's, in Reading, Pennsylvania, features packs of pretzels, candy, tortes, meats and cheeses.

The way in which food is normally bought in super-markets has already been covered, but an exception to their general hegemony is when you want ethnic ingredients, for, say, Japanese, Chinese, Korean or even Italian cooking. A limited range of these may be available in supermarkets, but for serious cooking you need a specialist shop, often in an ethnic part of town; there are actually ethnic supermarkets in areas heavily populated by a particular ethnic group, especially the various Oriental nations.

If you live in an agricultural area you can find roadside stands in profusion, selling local produce. In upstate New York, for example, you can buy grapes, apples, maple sugar, peaches and sometimes even wine from a roadside mer-chant. There are also 'farmers' markets' in many cities; for instance, there is a big one in downtown Los Angeles called Grand Central Market, where produce from the surrounding area is sold six days a week, all year round. The prices there are lower than in the supermarket, but the range of groceries may be more limited than in a supermarket, and you cannot select fruit and vegetables for yourself; you have to rely on the stallholder. Because farmers' markets are habitually patronised by those who care about good food, you can also find decent bread and a fair selection of cheeses in many of them, often at much lower prices than in supermarkets. The cheeses are sometimes nearing (or may even have passed) their 'sell-by' date, so check them carefully, but remember that our ancestors invented cheese mainly as a means of preserving milk-protein long after the milk had soured: unless they are actually mildewed, there is virtually nothing that is likely to have gone wrong with them.

Consumer goods, whether appliances such as stoves, washing machines and refrigerators, or leisure goods such as televisions, video recorders and home computers, are for the most part astonishingly cheap, though domestic pro-ducts are sometimes old-fashioned, not very competently styled, and even downright crude. Even so, consumer goods are one area where the wealth of the United States really makes itself obvious: the sheer size of the market makes possible tremendous economies of scale, and the high average incomes mean that the manufacturers can offer plenty of choice. The same is even true of motor-cars; the effective cost of a new car in the United States is considerably lower than in the UK, especially after you have made allowance for the very much better salaries.

An important point about motor-cars, though, is that the 'sticker price' in the showroom or in the advertisement may or may not reflect the actual price of the car on the road. The base model will be just about drivable; when the salesman starts listing the options, you may begin to wonder about whether you are paying extra for the wheels and the seats. The answer of course is that you may well be, if you want alloy wheels and leather seats. The options, both the ones you want and the ones which the car just 'happens' to come with, can add several hundred or even several thousand dollars to the price. This is admittedly true in the UK as well, though it does not take place to anything like the same extent, but it is one of the reasons why the Japanese have done so well in both markets: their cars come fully equipped, so you know what you are getting. In the United States, most domestic manufacturers stick to the old ways, but imports can vary considerably; a friend of the authors was considering a Mercedes-Benz and a Jaguar, which had similar sticker prices. Then she found that in order to get the things which were standard on the Jaguar (such as real leather seats, a sun roof, etc), the Mercedes cost over $5,000 extra . . .

Although most manufactured goods (except some European imports) are surprisingly cheap in the United States, the price of most services — professional and non-professional — is often hair-raising. The main non-professional services which are likely to concern our readers are those dealing with repairs and maintenance, especially of automobiles, though much of what follows will also apply to, for example, painters and decorators.

To begin with, as in Britain, it is not easy to find someone who is both reliable and competent. This is no particular reflection upon American craftsmen, many of whom are first-rate, but it does reflect upon American business methods which encourage 'cowboys'. In almost any field, the manufacturer or his appointed agents are likely to be by far the most reliable option, though their rates will often be so high as to make you gasp.

Secondly, competent independent workers are likely to be independent to the point of arrogance; if they have a good reputation, they are likely to have more work than they can handle, and because they know that to subcontract the work to someone less competent could ruin that reputation, they jack up their prices and time their work at *their* convenience, not yours. Plumbers are particularly notorious for this, though there are also signs of it developing in (of all things) the upper end of the laundry and dry-cleaning trade.

Thirdly, most Americans are in any case rather cavalier about maintenance. The old dictum, 'If it ain't broke, don't fix it' is applied particularly strongly to motor cars, which many people simply never service, even to change the oil: they just tip in more oil to bring the level up to the proper line on the dipstick. This was not too bad on the old V-8s, with their big, understressed, virtually indestructible engines, but it does not do European or Japanese imports any good at all, which is why it is as well to examine a used imported car very carefully indeed.

The American equivalent of a motor-car service is usually a 'tune-up', which is only performed when the car is running roughly. There are a number of tune-up chains throughout the country, where oil is changed and (in theory) plugs, points and timing are checked – though it is a common complaint that the car often runs worse *after* a 'tune-up' than before. Many of these chains employ essentially unskilled labour, taught to do a few simple tasks by rote, and so, regrettably, do some so-called 'repair' shops; Pirsig's *Zen and the Art of Motorcycle Maintenance* contains some real horror stories about this, as well as being a fascinating book about America.

The only real hope with independent contractors and repairers is to ask your friends whom they recommend, and if their recommendations are any good, to stick with that person. This is admittedly the same in Britain, but the vastly increased cost of labour in the United States makes it all the more important to check carefully. Alternatively, if you are on a comparatively short visit or will be returning to the UK at any time, you may wish to wait until you get home to get something fixed. More than once, the authors have bought cameras (especially Leicas) in the United States which were broken and beyond economic repair, only to have them fixed in the UK either for their personal use or for resale. One Leica IIIf which cost $100 to buy then cost £15 to fix, and (when we got tired of it) fetched £180 – a profit at the time of about £100.

It is something of a toss-up whether professional or non-professional services are proportionately more expensive; there are stories of doctors who became plumbers because although it did not pay quite so well, the overheads were far lower and the profits therefore higher. These may be apocryphal, but given that at the time of writing a doctor might typically pay $50,000 a year in malpractice and accident insurance (to which we shall return later), they are not impossible to believe.

Doctors' fees in the United States are legendary, and the explanations lie in several areas. First, a medical education is very expensive indeed, and the student may well go into debt to pay for it, so he or she has a large investment to recover. Secondly, people who are ill are very vulnerable until they are cured, and very grateful when they are, so the price is, as economists say, 'elastic'. Thirdly, most fees are paid by insurance companies, and although they do their best to pay out as little as possible, they know that if it came to a lawsuit between them and the doctor, the doctor would win, at least in a jury trial: no jury loves an insurance company. Fourthly, because Americans are so profoundly litigious, and willing to sue for staggering damages at the slightest excuse, doctors have to do a great deal which is not strictly medically necessary in order to cover themselves legally, as well as paying extremely high malpractice insurance, as already mentioned. Prices increase on the one hand because of the increased numbers of lab tests (themselves alarmingly expensive) and the need for second opinions, and on the other because of the high insurance payments.

Malpractice suits have reached such absurd levels in the United States that several states have introduced statutory limits for certain types of claims, and others will almost certainly follow. Things were so bad at the time of writing that insurance companies would almost automatically settle any claim for less than $10,000 out of court, because at this level fees would eat up just as much money and they knew that they would probably lose if the case came to court; the jury's reasoning would be (a) that doctors were a grasping bunch and that (b) even if the doctor were not at fault, the insurance company had plenty of money and could well afford to pay – without really reflecting on the fact that it was this sort of decision which drove up insurance premiums and hence doctors' bills!

In addition to doctors' bills, it is worth remembering that you have to pay the full cost of prescriptions. The rises in National Health prescription fees in the UK appear in a slightly different perspective when you realise that a single prescription of one of the more exotic antibiotics can easily be *ten times* as much as the National Health fee.

The position of dentists is very similar to that of doctors, and those who complain at British National Health charges should reflect that the maximum possible fee in the UK *for an entire course of treatment* is less than half of the cost of a single gold crown in the United States. Get your teeth fixed before you go!

Lawyers are scarcely less notorious. A major reason for this is that lawyers in the US are allowed to work on a contingent fee basis – no damages, no fee – which constitutes the crime of 'champerty' in the UK. The advantage of contingent fees is obvious, both to the lawyer and his or her client, but the disadvantage is that with, say, $100,000 or more riding on the judge's decision, the lawyer is no longer a 'friend of the court' as he or she is supposed to be, but rather an individual fighting desperately for his or her own money, and ethical standards can (and frequently do) suffer. And because so much money is available on contingent-fee cases, if you do have to hire a lawyer on a non-contingency basis, the fees expected are enormous.

Tax advisers and accountants are the other two types of professionals whom our readers may (and indeed should) encounter, and all that need be said about them is that their fees are rather higher than in the UK, even when the 'rule of two' is applied (the rule which states that the real purchasing power of the dollar is about half that of the pound sterling, regardless of the actual exchange rate), but not vastly so.

Paying for things in the United States may bring some surprises, too. To begin with, prices are normally quoted and marked *exclusive* of sales tax – the equivalent of VAT, though usually much lower. To make life interesting, though, not all items are taxable, and exactly what is taxable varies from state to state. The anomalies in the system were made abundantly clear a few years ago, when California noticed that nuts were taxed, while candy was not. On the perfectly rational grounds that nuts are better for you than candy, candy was then taxed while nuts were exempted! It is not easy to work out what the tax will be, either, even if you know what is taxed and what is not: in Los Angeles, there is a 6 per cent state tax plus a 0.5 per cent city tax, and if you can work out 6.5 per cent of $1.36 in your head without concentrating you're a better man than we are, Gunga Din. Sales taxes vary throughout the country, and *may in certain cases be payable on private sales*; for example, in California, cars, motor-homes, boats and (apparently) aircraft are taxable, so that if you sell or buy a car for $5,000, then $300 will be payable on top of that in sales tax. Sales tax is normally paid by the buyer when he or she goes to re-register the vehicle in question.

Contrary to popular belief, cash is still accepted in America, and is certainly better received than cheques, which are normally accepted by professionals, and may be accepted in stores, but are seldom even considered in restaurants. If you want to pay by cheque, you will probably be asked to present a driver's licence and at least one other form of identification (you will usually be asked, 'Have you got another ID?'). They may also ask for your employer's name and 'phone number. The cheque, which must be drawn on a local, or at least an in-state bank, must be imprinted in magnetic ink with your name, address, 'phone number and account number (some cheques even show their owner's driver's licence number). Not all retailers will be this strict, but the majority will. Most states impose legal penalties to discourage bounced cheques; for instance, in California you may be liable for up to three times the value of the cheque, or $100, whichever is greater. All retailers charge a fee for a returned cheque, often as much as $10 for every time a cheque must be re-presented, and then there is the bank's re-presentation fee as well.

Traveller's cheques, however, are accepted almost everywhere as readily as cash. You may have to show some ID, but there will be a great deal less trouble than with a personal cheque.

Although credit cards are popular and very easy to get, their use is not quite as widespread as you may have been led to believe. In addition to the major cards, such as Visa, Mastercard (Access), American Express and Diners' Club, many retailers also issue their own cards. The larger department stores almost all do, as do most of the petrol companies, and indeed some will only accept their own cards.

116

There are also surprisingly many places which do not accept cards at all, including many petrol stations, and it is as well to check before you make your purchase. In gas stations in many places, it is also perfectly usual for there to be a surcharge of around a nickel (5c) a gallon. Visa is easily the most useful single card, closely followed by Mastercard/Access, but you cannot rely automatically on their being accepted, and you should always check before attempting to make a purchase: unlike most of Europe, there may not be stickers or placards advertising the cards which are accepted, especially in motels.

A recent problem with credit cards has been that people will obtain account numbers from the sales slip carbons, which they pull out of merchants' trash bins, and use them to order goods and services by 'phone or mail. Because of this, most salespeople, waitresses and the like will offer the carbons from your charge slip for you to destroy.

11

Business Life

Business life in America is a hard school. Despite a considerable softening of attitudes throughout the century, and a patchwork of often inadequately thought-out laws governing, for example, the employment of racial minorities, or safety standards, capitalism is alive and well and living in America — and still pretty much red in tooth and claw. Although there is a marked difference between Eastern and Western attitudes, to which we shall return later, the general rule throughout the country is long hours and short holidays.

Typical office hours are 9am to 5pm, as in the UK, and lunch is usually taken in two shifts, except for the most senior personnel: the first shift will usually be from noon to 1pm, and the second from 1pm to 2pm. You may or may not have much say in which shift you take. The reason the hours seem long, though, is the rigorous timekeeping which is taken for granted in the US: 'clocking in' (and out) is regarded as perfectly normal, even for middle management, and at lunchtime you are expected to be at your desk until the last minute and back in the same chair one hour later. Almost nowhere is there the five or ten minutes' grace which is taken for granted (provided it is not abused) in the UK, and a couple of hours off to go to the dentist, or whatever, is normally taken as a half day from the annual sick-leave or even personal-leave allowance. The standard working week is still forty hours in many places, too, not the thirty-eight or thirty-seven hours that it is in the UK.

Although this sort of timekeeping is no more than what is *supposed* to happen in the UK, the real shock (if you are used to an easygoing business environment) comes with the holidays. In addition to the six statutory holidays a year —

(*right*) The West, Colorado — wild sunflowers and a deserted road

the equivalent of British Bank Holidays – most companies will have a couple of days' 'floating' holidays, determined by the company in some cases or the employee in others, depending on the company. Otherwise, you can expect a maximum of two weeks (ie ten days) personal leave in the first year you work for a company, with an increment of a day or two per year for each year thereafter – and some companies only allow one week (five days) in the first year, or even no holiday at all, though this may either jump to two weeks in the second year or still be subject to gradual increments.

What is worse, the six statutory holidays are by no means all 'long weekends'. Christmas Day, New Year's Day and Independence Day (the Fourth of July) can obviously fall on any day of the week; Thanksgiving is the fourth Thursday in November; while only Memorial Day (the last Monday in May) and Labor Day (the first Monday in September) always allow long weekends. Traditionally, Memorial Day Weekend and Labor Day Weekend mark the beginning and end of the vacation season, and all resorts (and roads) are impossibly crowded on these days, so you might as well stay at home anyway.

Of course, things are not always this bad. Some companies will make up the odd day between Thanksgiving and the weekend, and if Christmas falls on a Tuesday or Thursday, they will throw in the Monday or Friday as appropriate. On the other hand, the situation in retail trading can be worse! Shops stay open not only on Sundays but also on most of the statutory holidays (though not normally Christmas Day and New Year's Day). Typically, the 'coal-face' sales staff are paid overtime rates, and work fairly normal hours (say 8.45am to 5.45pm): they are then heavily supplemented by part-timers after those hours and on Sundays and

(*above left*) Berthoud Pass: this picture is self-explanatory, but it is fascinating to know that within a few miles of this sign, you can actually *see* rivers forming a couple of hundred yards apart which will drain into the Pacific on one side, and the Atlantic on the other

(*below left*) Secret Service car: every now and then you run across something which really makes you realise how different America is from anywhere in Europe – and indeed, which makes you wonder if Americans have not somehow missed the point. Where else would you dream of finding a car *admitting* that it belongs to the *uniformed* branch of the Secret Service?

statutory holidays. Middle managers, and even some senior managers, have as a condition of their employment the obligation to stay late a couple of evenings a week, though rarely, if at all, on Sundays.

Nor is sick leave any more generous. Often, a firm will allow absolutely no paid sick leave for the first three months, after which they will give perhaps five days a year, again subject to annual increments in most cases. Any additional time spent off sick will be unpaid.

Of course, if you are sufficiently senior, you may be able to negotiate a better package, and if you are changing companies at a high enough level you should be able to carry your leave and other allowances over into your new job. It is, however, very important to establish leave allowances, even if you are working for a British company, as they may not be anything like what you expect.

Of the various 'fringe benefits' which you should also investigate, health insurance is the most important. The elderly are entitled to Social Security and Medicare, but this is on a contributory basis, and you must have worked (and paid in) for forty quarter-years. Otherwise, charity hospitals are very basic, and getting a reasonable standard of medical care means spending a lot of money. Some idea of prices is given in the previous chapter, and medical insurance plans vary widely.

Few employers offer 100 per cent coverage for the whole family, though some do (notably those who are posting their employees overseas for a fixed term), so it becomes a matter of looking at the exclusions. Typically, pre-existing conditions will be excluded by the insurers, no matter who is paying, and even if the company pays the entire premium, this may not cover the entire cost of treatment. A typical arrangement would mean that the employing company, via their insurers, would pay 80 per cent of all hospital bills up to a set limit – perhaps $10,000 at the time of writing – and then 100 per cent beyond that. You would then be personally responsible for the remainder of the bill, though you might also be able to take out secondary insurance to pay some or all of that: secondary insurers will normally only pay out if the primary insurers have already done so, and this is by no means always certain, as American insurers will do their very best to wriggle out of paying anything, as already noted in the chapter on transport. Note too that dental and optical insurance may not be included in health insurance, and that some plans exclude pregnancy.

This is, however, only one possible example. Percentages might differ; you might be required to pay a part of the premium; there might be an absolute limit on the amount which the insurers will pay in any one year; you may be obliged to pay, say, the first $200 in any one year; the insurance may only cover you, and not your spouse, or you and your spouse but not your children; and there is almost certain to be a waiting period of at least one month, and possibly as much as six months, before you are covered at all. In this case, you may well be able to arrange temporary insurance in the UK, but you must do so before you go.

Pension plans are something else to consider. If your employers' pension insurers have a subsidiary or an associate company in the UK, you may be able to transfer pension rights when you return there; you may be able to recover a lump sum at the end of your employment in the US; or you may simply get nothing. There may also be tax-shelter savings plans, often known as 'thrift' plans, whereby a proportion of your salary is deducted and put in a savings scheme before tax is assessed; in this case you cannot usually get at the money for several years, and there are (as the small print invariably says) 'substantial penalties for early withdrawal', because you will have to pay tax, though you may be able to borrow against the security of your untouchable money. Some companies can also arrange for IRA (Individual Retirement Account) payments to be deducted from your pay before you get it; for further details on IRAs, see Chapter 14.

Some companies also offer profit-sharing schemes, sometimes in the form of stock-purchasing schemes with the company contributing a percentage of the cost of the stock. Like the thrift plans, this money is usually deducted before you see your paycheck.

Company cars are much less widespread in the US than in the UK, though employers may expect you to use your car on their business, in which case you should check the insurance position carefully; most employers will have a policy specifically covering this, but demand to see it if you have any doubts.

Only in the uppermost reaches of a very few companies are such benefits as assistance with children's education to be found, and even there they are rare. This is largely due to the American tax system, which is described at greater length below. At the other end of the scale, Luncheon Vouchers are not widespread, either.

In short, American companies may pay well, but they expect a lot in return for their money, and the lack of fringe benefits may mean that there are hidden costs for which you had not allowed. In large part, this is due to the strain of Puritanism which still runs broad and deep in the United States; the Protestant Work Ethic really means something to most people. On the other hand, its influence is much more obvious in the East, where enjoying yourself, especially when you are working, is often seen as akin to spitting on Calvin's grave. It is at its most obvious in banking and finance, where things are sometimes grotesquely old-fashioned, and in these fields it can be seen all over the country, but in manufacturing industries there is a vastly more casual attitude in the West, especially in the newer high-tech Sunbelt industries: the laid-back attitudes of Silicon Valley (Santa Clara) in California are legendary, and many people believe that this is the direction in which the 'post-industrial society' is moving. Similarly, standards of dress and address (though not of service) usually grow increasingly casual as you move westwards, though an overstuffed American maître d'hôtel in one of the more pompous Los Angeles restaurants is a wonderful parody of formality.

You should not, however, be deceived by even Silicon Valley casualness, where the boss may come to work in jeans, a T-shirt and bare feet. The 'bottom line' is still all-important in American business, and unless the company is making money at such a rate that the company does not really care about losing the odd few hundred (or thousand) dollars here and there, it is likely that your performance will be every bit as closely monitored as in a stuffy New England bank. Unless you are pulling your weight, you will be got rid of without further ado in either establishment: American companies are not slow to 'let people go', or (in plain English) to fire them. To be sure, there are American companies where there is dead wood, and where losses are being made; but, usually, these are either in the so-called 'sunset' manufacturing industries where the United States is falling behind other nations with a cheaper labour force, or in companies where the accountants are so preoccupied with the 'bottom line' that they have lost sight of how the company actually earns its money, and put all their energy into financial juggling.

This point about 'sunrise' and 'sunset' industries is one which has been made elsewhere, and which is probably equally true of the UK, but it is still worth stressing that neither sunrise nor sunset is as smooth and uniform a process as the words imply. Sunrises sometimes go out with a bang, or a whimper, and sunsets can behave like dying fireworks, kicking up a magnificent performance for quite a while before they finally go cold – and then providing another fizzle even when you thought they had died. To take specific examples, sunrise electronics companies and software houses are born and die every day, lasting anything from a few weeks to a few years, whereas the apparently sunset industry of motorcycle manufacture limps and staggers, then regains its strength to such good effect that it looks set to go on for ever – albeit with the help of a protectionist surcharge on imported bikes over 700cc (the smallest Harley is 883cc). American industry is constantly hollering for protectionist policies when they keep out foreign competition, but loud whining noises are heard when other countries impose tariff barriers which harm American export prospects.

In any industry, though, the Briton is likely to be extremely well received. The American stereotype of the Briton is that he or she is reserved to the point of coldness, very formal and possibly rather dour. Fortunately, if this is what is called for, most Britons can live up to the part rather well: a British accent conveys a great deal of formality and correctness to most Americans, and provided you refrain from four-letter words and deliberate Americanisms, you will be seen to be living the part. Dressing soberly, and affecting a somewhat John Bullish stance on international politics (and any other topic of conversation, for that matter) will reinforce the image; so will driving a British car, as already mentioned.

In practice, though, it is hard to tell whether the British are more surprised at the American (and specifically Eastern) talent for formality, or the Americans are more surprised at the British talent for informality, and indeed for matching or exceeding the most laid-back of Californian attitudes. In the East, or in a more formal environment elsewhere in the country, many Americans will be surprised at how cordial you can be, while still remaining British; in the Sunbelt, you can relax as much as you like (always subject to that 'bottom line', at least at work) and they will love you for it. It really is astonishing how often people say, 'I had no idea that British people were so warm and friendly,' either when they come back from a European vacation or when they are talking of their British colleagues.

It is also possible to reinforce your good image without too much effort. For example, British suits have a considerable cachet, even if they are slightly out of style (this merely reinforces your image as a Sound Citizen). The same is true of British shirts, ties and shoes. Being seen reading one of the British 'quality' papers, marks you out as a person who likes to consider things judiciously; driving a Jaguar shows that you appreciate standards of both comfort and handling to which the New World cannot aspire. If you want to be a real John Bull, refer to the United States as 'the Colonies'; most Americans, far from being offended, will be delighted – though you have to know them well before you point out that from the British point of view, George Washington, Paul Revere and the others were a bunch of terrorists.

Image is not everything, though, and your first experiences of American business ethics may leave you thoroughly alarmed. Many Americans are honourable people, whose word is as good as their bond; others are honourable people with whom (in the words of Sam Goldwyn), 'a verbal contract isn't worth the paper it is written on'; and some are just plain villains. In a field which the authors know well, publishing, it is by no means unknown for a publisher to string along a packager (the person who actually produces the book) until printing time, when they will turn around and offer perhaps 50 per cent of the amount they were originally discussing, knowing that the packager will be forced to accept if only to cut his or her losses. The attitude of insurers has already been mentioned, and scandals about overcharging on defence contracts were almost a way of life throughout the 1980s. In general, unless something is *in writing*, and unless that writing has been scrutinised by your lawyers, it is very unwise indeed to rely upon it.

The unfortunate result (or cause) of all this is that American business is, for the most part, based on distrust – and this applies at every stage of the business. At its most trivial, it is seen in the requirement in many places that you pay for gas before pumping it, or in the way that many stores require you either to check your bags in with Security or allow them to be searched; when the authors suggested to a doorman that if K-Mart (a particularly cheap store) was not prepared to trust them not to slip things into their camera bags, they were not prepared to entrust $3,000 worth of Leica cameras to K-Mart, K-Mart was Not Amused. In fact, this brings up an issue of mistrust which amounts almost to paranoia: some stores refuse to allow any cameras inside, on the grounds that they might be used for photographing the interior and planning a robbery!

The list of examples could be multiplied indefinitely. To take another example which the authors know well, a used camera is usually guaranteed for six months in the UK: in the US, ninety days is the maximum, thirty days is usual, and seven days (or no guarantee at all) is not unheard of. Again, many firms refuse to refund cash for faulty merchandise, but will only issue a credit slip – a restriction which is illegal in Britain (and in parts of the US too, for that matter). Of course, the law varies from state to state, but it pays to read the terms and conditions of sale very carefully, and to insist on your legal rights if necessary.

At the beginning of the chapter, we referred to the 'patchwork of often inadequately thought-out laws', and a couple of examples of these will show what we mean. Although warranties may be very limited, there are truly hair-raising product-liability, personal-liability and consequential-loss laws in many states. Some of these may be expressly limited, though others may not, so warnings are printed on the most unlikely things: for example, cheap American 'champagne' (actually produced by the Charmat bulk process, but still very drinkable) has a warning printed on the seal, to the effect that the contents are under pressure, and you should point the cork away from your eyes when opening the bottle! Signs specifically warning against diving into shallow (private!) swimming pools are commercially available, lest some idiot dive into your 3ft deep pool, break his neck, and then sue you on the grounds that you should have warned him not to. Even American football helmets carry warnings that using them to 'butt, ram or spear' an opponent could injure him severely. Perhaps the high-water mark of this lunacy was the suit brought by a burglar who fell through a skylight and severely injured himself, *while trying to burgle the premises.* That such a suit should be brought at all is extraordinary; that he should win it (which he did) is incredible. As remarked in the last chapter, Americans are a profoundly litigious race, and will sue you as soon as look at you.

On another topic, federal law requires (or required) all employers to show the racial background of their employees, for statistical purposes, on certain Federal Bureau of Statistics forms. Unfortunately, it is illegal to ask the employee for this information, at least before you employ him or her, and although it may be legal to ask afterwards, he or she is specifically legally exempted from having to answer. Better still, it is illegal to employ illegal immigrants, but it is also illegal to ask if they are illegal immigrants . . .

This does not mean however that you can easily get work as an illegal immigrant, as employers *are* allowed to ask you for your Social Security number, and you are legally obliged to give it to them. In order to get a Social Security number, you have to show the Social Security office your passport, and they will not give you one if you do not have a work permit. You can fudge it for a few weeks, or even a few months if you are lucky, but Uncle Sam will catch you sooner or later.

American insecurity also spills over into banking, though curiously, most banking halls in the US are open, airy places where there is no bulletproof glass between customer and staff, just a modest wooden counter. There is however normally an armed guard on duty! For most people, the important point is that it is actually *illegal* to go overdrawn, or at least to exceed your agreed overdraft limit, and that this can be regarded as a very serious offence indeed. A bounced cheque will cost you a good deal more than in the UK – in California, for example, a 1985 statute made the drawer of a rubber cheque liable for three times the face value of the cheque, or $100, whichever was greater, quite apart from the bank's re-presentation fee – and it can also wreck your creditworthiness quite quickly.

In the US, credit is generally much more closely monitored than in the UK, and it is by no means unusual for a bit of 'snooping' to be done in addition to the investigation you expect – namely, a letter to your bank manager. Several companies maintain blacklists of poor credit risks, and (as in the UK) it is possible to get on these by accident, without knowing who it is that is wrecking your credit. New federal law makes it easier for you to find out, but it is as well to pay your bills reasonably promptly, or you will find yourself running out of credit. It is also extremely difficult for new arrivals in the country to get credit, unless they can show glowing references from their employer, and it is next to impossible for freelances to get a good 'line of credit' (the standard term in the United States) because everything is geared towards the employee, though sight of your income tax returns may convince them.

The rather surprising converse of this is that because creditworthiness checks are so rigorous, many institutions are constantly pushing credit at you. The availability of credit cards has been mentioned in the last chapter, and bank loans and loans from Savings and Loan companies are also constantly advertised. It is worth noting that all serious banks are members of the Federal Deposit Insurance Corporation, which is a federal insurance scheme guaranteeing the deposits of all but the very largest investors (at the time of writing, up to $100,000), while Savings and Loans are not necessarily so insured with the Federal Savings and Loan Insurance Corporation, which performs a similar function to the FDIC, and can (and do) crash. A Savings and Loan is rather akin to a British Building Society.

At the time of writing, there were no restrictions on the free movement of capital in or out of either the United States or the United Kingdom, at least not until you are talking about corporate millions, though there are limits on the amount of *cash* you can move – the US limit, for example, stood at $5,000 for some years. This can of course change at any time. Arrangements can normally be made easily enough for really long stays, or for business trips, but long vacations are another matter.

The easiest way to transfer money is probably telegraphically – the charge for this is very modest – but you may also wish to use banker's drafts at first, which may be bought either in dollars or in pounds sterling, if you are using a new bank or a new branch. If you are living in the United States for any length of time, you may find it more convenient to open an account with an American bank, simply because there are more branches, and because you can use the money 'magic machines' (though British Visa cards are increasingly being integrated into the American automatic-teller system; late 1986 is the target date for full integration of all Visa systems), but it is probably useful to keep your UK account, if only for trips home. It is also convenient to be able to pay UK bills at a time when the dollar is strong, and US bills at a time when it is weak!

Of course, if you earn money, you will be taxed on it. The rules concerning how long you must be in the United States before being liable for tax are given in Chapter 3; under certain conditions, you may be able to avoid US tax and pay UK tax instead – and even though US tax rates are generally lower, it is worth paying UK tax if you possibly can. The reason for this is simple: it keeps you clear of the immense complications and potentially extremely unpleasant penalties which Uncle Sam imposes on his hapless income-tax payers.

To begin with, the tax is paid differently. There is a form of PAYE, but it is based on your estimate of what your allowances will be for the coming year; a proportion of your salary is withheld upon that basis – and, to make things more complicated, tax is computed on the basis of a (very variable) percentage, *plus a flat fee* which varies according to your income! At the end of the tax year, which is mercifully a calendar year instead of the odd British period, you have to fill in a massive and complicated form with the *actual* amounts which these allowances added up to. The difference between what has actually been withheld and what should have been withheld is then either payable, or refunded, as appropriate.

This does not sound too complex, but the trouble is that there are so many allowances, and such strict interpretation of what may or may not be allowed within each category, that the whole process becomes immensely complicated, and it becomes virtually essential for most people (even employees) to hire an accountant. There is admittedly a 'short form', but this is only applicable if you have no deductions or complications of any kind, such as interest payable or mortgages, or income from stock. In fact, part of President Reagan's platform for re-election was simplification and rationalisation of the American tax system, though at the time of writing this was bogged down by a mass of conflicting special-interest lobbies. To quote only one of the more bizarre intricacies, far from paying tax on their riches, oilmen could claim a tax *loss* because their valuable oil asset (which by definition is non-renewable) was being depleted by their selling it!

Even this would not be so bad if it were not for the powers of the Internal Revenue Service, the IRS. Although they are usually charming and helpful people, the powers which they can command if they wish are awesome. They can investigate almost anything, and if they do a full-scale audit, they can demand that you produce receipts or other written evidence to support *all* your tax claims for the past *seven years*. Consequently, most people are very frightened of the IRS, which is quite unfair as they will usually do their best to explain things and to help you to comply with the law (which is horribly complicated); this 'reign of terror' image is, however, hard to dispel, in the light of those massive powers.

The net result of all this is that most people – the 'little guys' – are very honest with their taxes, while the big wheeler-dealers (and we are talking in millions now, not in salaries) hire lawyers to do their rule-bending for them, and accountants to bury the evidence. Many people also suspect that the IRS will occasionally audit a 'little guy' for no particular reason, just to maintain the balance of terror, though on strictly personal acquaintance the authors find this hard to believe. What actually happens is that all returns are subject to random examination, and if the spot check turns up cause for suspicion, the IRS may well decide to audit.

One thing that is certain, though, is that the IRS makes far fewer allowances for human frailty, and far fewer trade-offs and compromises of the 'Oh well, it's only a couple of quid either way' variety than the British tax authorities. They want accuracy to the nearest dollar (you are allowed to round off cents!) and if they don't get it, they can make life difficult.

Your troubles do not end, however, with satisfying the IRS. In many states, there is also *local* income tax. The rate of tax is very much lower than the federal rate, which is itself lower than British tax, and the two together probably do not amount to as much as Her Majesty's Tax Inspectors take from you, but you have a whole second set of income-tax forms to file, though they are mercifully less complicated than the federal version. State tax inspectors are nothing like as heavy as the IRS, as a rule, but they do have reciprocal agreements with the IRS, so both sets of figures had better agree! The administration of the tax works in the same way as federal tax.

The only other government deduction is Social Security, which at the time of writing was 7–8 per cent of salary (with an upper limit, which is very high indeed) deducted to provide an old-age pension and Medicare; it appears on your pay-slip as FICA (Federal Insurance Contribution Act). You usually only become eligible for these when you are sixty-five, though Medicare benefits are available to certain groups (war veterans, the disabled, etc) at a lower age. Under reciprocal agreements between the United States and the United Kingdom, it is possible to pay UK National Insurance Contributions in the US, and US Social Security in the UK for that matter, for up to three years: after that, you must join the system of the country in which you are working.

In many states there is also a State Disability Insurance scheme, which is (once more) compulsory, and which removes a further small percentage of your salary to provide a disability allowance. This allowance is payable after seven days off work, though the period may be varied, and is payable for as long as you cannot work. Once again, there is an upper limit to this deduction, and it is a good deal lower than the Social Security upper limit. In those states where no such scheme operates, disability insurance is offered privately at similar rates.

12
Relaxation

After the last chapter, it may seem that you are going to have precious little time for relaxation, but although your vacations may be severely curtailed, you will still have evenings, weekends and the occasional long weekend, the American equivalent of a British bank holiday – although Memorial Day weekend and Labor day weekend generally place such a strain on every tourist facility and attraction in the United States that you may prefer to stay home.

Beginning with your evenings, there is of course television – which has already been pretty thoroughly damned in Chapter 2. On the bright side, though, there are usually many more channels to choose from, and if you have a weakness for (say) *M.A.S.H.* or *Star Trek* or even *Doctor Who*, you can usually find at least one channel that is repeating them that day. Better still, there are several sub-scription-only channels where for a comparatively modest fee (about the price of three or four movie tickets a month) you can see both first-run (current-release) and 'classic' movies, as well as (fairly soft) pornography if your tastes run that way. Most subscription channels run a couple of late-night porno double bills each week, but in New York City there is said to be a channel which shows nothing but. At the other extreme, there are Southern Baptist and other religious channels where you can rely on religious ranting for up to twenty-four hours a day. The local public-service channel can usually be relied upon to show a fair sprinkling of the better British programmes too, and you'll find that many Americans have a terrible weakness for Benny Hill.

Likewise, American radio often has little to offer, though public-service radio is generally worth listening to and there may be major concerts (either live or on record) sponsored by large corporations; these may (or may not!) rival the BBC.

When it comes to going out, American theatre is usually of a very high standard indeed – in the major cities, often well above London standards – but prices are even more hair-raising than in Britain, frequently twice or three times as high even after you have made allowance for the exchange rate. Furthermore, it is only in the biggest cities that you will see much modern, experimental, or even recent theatre: out in the sticks, as in many provincial theatres in the UK, the staples are the time-worn 'classics' and musicals. Intriguingly, community non-professional theatre (the 'amateur dramatics' of Britain) is often of astonishing quality, again in the bigger cities: it is often of a standard which would put to shame many professional British repertory companies. From the point of view of both the audience and the would-be performer, technician or director, community theatre can be a very rewarding experience.

Substantially the same is true of classical music concerts as of professional theatre, though (as in Britain) opera only makes its way to a very few theatres. Pop concerts tend to be even bigger than in the UK, with even heavier and uglier bouncers, and at even higher prices, so they are generally less attractive.

On the last of the 'cultural' entertainments, some of the finest art galleries and museums in the world are in the United States, with sheer buying power in many cases compensating for the centuries over which some European collections were formed. The Getty museums are famous, of course, and there are countless others, from faultless displays of some of the loveliest things in the world to 'mathom houses', to borrow a Hobbit word. (Tolkien readers may recall that 'mathoms' are things which nobody particularly wants, but which are too good to throw away.) Many small museums in the United States are wonderful mathom houses; the museum of the gold-mining days at Angel's Camp in California immediately springs to mind.

On less exalted planes, there are the cinemas, restaurants and bars. Cinemas in the United States are much the same as in the UK, with strictly comparable prices (which means that prices are quite low, from an American point of view), but they do not show so many double bills (the British practice is a hangover from the days of 'quota quickies', when a certain percentage of films shown had to be British) and smoking is not permitted in the auditorium in most (possibly all) states. Many US-made films are released several weeks, or even months, earlier in the US than in Britain, which is good for scoring points off your friends at home.

The whole subject of restaurants is an enormously complex one. To begin with, eating out is much more usual in the United States than in Britain, and as a result there is a much greater variety of all kinds of restaurants in all price ranges. There is, however, a sharp dividing line between pretentious and unpretentious restaurants. The vast majority are unpretentious, but the pretentious ones (which are principally, though by no means exclusively, found in Los Angeles and New York) are very much on the British pattern for the same type of place: grossly overpriced, especially on the wine list, grossly over-formal (in that they require collars and ties and jackets), and from a gastronomic point of view distinctly unimpressive. To be sure, there are a few good, formal, expensive restaurants, but they are no more common than they are in London. If you move in the appropriate circles, you will no doubt rapidly learn which are worth while and which are not; otherwise, you can have a lot more fun with the unpretentious places.

The standard American meal is of course a steak, and steak houses of various types and qualities exist all over America; there are certain rural areas, especially in the Midwest, where you will find very little else except perhaps lobster tails and some rather tired fish. American restaurants almost invariably overcook fish, and are also much given to frying fish which most people would regard as more fit for steaming or grilling, so except in New England (and as far down as Delaware) or in a few specialty restaurants on the West Coast, you might as well abandon the idea of fish. Nor should you rely on being able to get a rare steak: although Texans are fond of boasting about eating whole steers raw, and California and New York City understand *bleu*, 'rare' elsewhere is likely to range from medium-rare to medium. Why this should be, when so many Americans cook superb rare steaks at home, is not clear, but it happens.

It is not always predictable, either, whether you will be able to get a drink with your meal. Whole tracts of the United States are legally 'dry', and others are effectively so, so it is always as well to inquire, before you sit down, whether they serve wine and beer. Sometimes the answer will be a shocked 'No!', as though you were a degenerate even to ask.

If you do order a drink, it is generally far better to order the house carafe wine than to order a European import or a domestic varietal wine, unless you are trying to impress someone, preferably with the aid of an expense account – and given the present climate of opinion in America about alcohol, you may impress them more by ordering Perrier water. Californian reds, in particular, can rival all but the very best French vins de table, and will certainly be better than the majority of French imports on the wine-list, except in the most expensive places. Gallo's Hearty Burgundy, for example, may sound like Wino's Delight, but it is a first-class everyday wine which the authors would drink in England if only they could get it. Domestic varietals are very variable: the best, such as the better Cabernet Sauvignons, are excellent, while others are very ordinary indeed. The price, however, is not so variable: in a restaurant, a decent domestic varietal wine will cost as much as a good import, which is three to five times as much as the Gallo brothers' superb plonk.

Domestic beer is almost without exception weak and served ice cold, in 12oz glasses if on draught or in 12oz bottles otherwise; if you want a decent quantity, order a pitcher, which can be anything from 48 to 64 fluid ounces. Draught normally tastes better than bottled, but as American beer can legally contain cereals other than barley and is almost never brewed stronger than 3.2 per cent alcohol, it is unlikely to appeal to the serious beer drinker. Imports are a much better proposition: Japanese beer is particularly good, as is Canadian beer, and Mexican beer is fairly good. There are various British imports, plus Guinness, but they are usually served ice cold too: specify a warm one if you do not want a nasty surprise. Of domestic beers, try (if you can) San Francisco's Anchor Steam and the various brews of New York State's Genesee Ales.

Although there are many different types of ethnic restaurant in the United States, of which we shall say more later, the typical American restaurant is a 'family' institution. It is something which is not anything like as common in Britain; perhaps the nearest equivalent is a Berni Inn, where the food is predictable and good (if rarely outstanding) and reasonably and predictably priced. Many of these restaurants are part of chains, which will be as standardised as possible throughout the country. Some are better than others: Denny's is regarded as the most basic sort of place that most people would want to eat (though it is still perfectly comfortable), while Sizzlers and Marie Callender's are a cut or two (or three) above, and the Velvet Turtle or a Hungry Tiger is a notch up again. At the other extreme, MacDonalds is well known for the qualities (good and not so good) for which it is known in Britain, and Carl's Junior is about the same. The ambience of all of these places is somewhere between that of a motorway service-area dining room and the sort of pub which has well-upholstered plastic seats, or possibly a Berni Inn or one of its imitators.

They are however usually surprisingly good value for money, and quite often there will be some 'all you can eat' dishes: Sizzler's all-you-can-eat salad and soup bar is a good example, with an excellent salad bar, which always includes fresh fruit as well (especially melon, watermelon, sliced fresh pineapple and so forth) and may include such items as whole avocados, seafood salad and potato skins, as well as bean sprouts, alfalfa sprouts, lettuce, spinach salad, tomato, radishes, spring and sweet onions, potato salad, grated cheese, crumbled bacon, sunflower seeds and croutons. The only drawback is the salad dressings, which are usually unappetisingly sweet: American 'French' dressing is not a simple vinegar-and-oil mix, but also contains sugar, tomato purée and herbs. 'Italian' dressing is usually vinegar-and-oil with herbs, but if you ask for a vinegar-and-oil dressing you will usually get mostly vinegar. There are usually three soups at Sizzler's, one of them a seafood soup or (on Fridays) clam chowder, and you can take as much as you like each time and return as often as you like.

While these places are fine for family dining, eating for fun usually involves going either to a good steak house (see above) or to an ethnic restaurant. Although there are proportionately far fewer Indian restaurants in the United States than in the UK, and rather fewer Greek, there are endless others to choose from. The authors have experienced Abyssinian, Chinese (both Cantonese and Szechuan), Filipino, German, Italian (including pizza parlours), Japanese, Laotian, Thai, Vietnamese and Yugoslav, and have wondered about Afghan, Lebanese, Turkish and countless others. Of all these, the two which we habitually patronise most are Japanese restaurants and pizza parlours.

The anaemic and shrunken pizzas commonly encountered in England cannot prepare you for the massive American deep-dish pizza, an inch deep in sausage, pepperoni, Mozarella and tomato sauce and commonly available in 'small' (feeds 1–2), 'medium' (feeds 2–3) and 'large' (feeds up to 6). Extremely reasonably priced, a good pizza is both delicious and fun; with a pitcher of beer or a carafe of red wine, it is for friends, lovers or the just plain hungry.

For a romantic evening, on the other hand, pizza may be a bit too hearty. Then, consider Japanese food. *Sushi* and *sashimi*, raw fish with and without a little rice pedestal, has to be experienced to be believed: it is stunningly delicious. Whether you opt for this or for cooked food (*tempura, yaki-soba* and so forth) or for a combination of both, the surroundings and service in a Japanese restaurant are wonderful; accompany the meal with hot *sake* in tiny bottles, and the experience is magical. For true addicts of Japanese food, who are prepared to forego some of the magic in return for more food, there are also all-you-can-eat sushi houses, which are a memorable event!

We have already more than touched upon the subject of bars and drinking, and this is the place to enlarge upon the subject. Throughout the first half of the 1980s, anti-liquor sentiment was growing stronger, and it was still growing as this book went to press. Alcoholics Anonymous became a favoured place for actors to meet agents and directors. The argument often voiced was that drunk driving was 'an increasing menace', but there were no convincing statistics to back up the allegation. Police found drunks an easy (and legitimate) target, though: increasingly, you could see drivers standing handcuffed beside their cars, where they had been stopped for a minor traffic violation and then breath-tested – although, interestingly, the blood alcohol limit in most states is 100mg per 100ml, 25 per cent higher than in most of Europe. Drunken teenage drivers were cited most of all, though it never seemed to occur to MADD (Mothers Against Drunk Driving) that it is much easier to control the access of teenagers to cars than the access of teenagers to alcohol, and that a dozen sixteen-year-olds thoroughly drunk, but without a car between them, were safer than a single sixteen-year-old trying to impress his girl-friend with his driving even when completely sober.

The bars are mostly dives, as already mentioned: they are murky, expensive places dedicated to getting drunk or (occasionally) to picking up members of the opposite sex (or the same sex). There are very few places which offer the same sort of comforts and amenities as a British pub, which may be one of the reasons why dining out is so popular: it replaces going out for a pint. Most women would not feel comfortable going into a bar alone unless they were out to be picked up, though (as already mentioned) some cocktail bars are more congenial.

Spirits, and the excellent wines of California, and the weak local beers, are cheap if you buy them in the supermarkets: getting drunk is not expensive, though it may be time-consuming if you want to do it on beer. Beer is treated more or less as a soft drink, which is appropriate enough, but *a glass* of wine with a meal is regarded as an adequate quantity by many, and as too much by some; American matrons giggle in Paris when a quarter-litre of wine is *compris* in the menu, and the idea of half a bottle or even a bottle of wine per person being a fit accompaniment for a meal is extraordinary to almost everyone. On the other hand, 'cocktails' (a limited range of mixed drinks, usually decep-tively innocuous-tasting) are poured down like water before a meal in some circles. The art of drinking steadily but slowly through an evening, or a cocktail party, and maintaining a slight merriment without actually becoming drunk, scarcely exists: in the American navy, there is a widespread belief that the Royal Navy organises its parties into Port and Starboard Watches, and that the first watch retires intoxi-cated half way through the party, leaving the other to drink their American guests under the table. Americans have always been like this: the reason why the American navy is 'dry' to this day is that at the historic engagement between the *Chesapeake* and the *Shannon*, the Americans were so drunk that the English hardly had to fight at all.

Prohibition may seem to be a part of history now, but it is always close under the surface. The drinking age is gradually being standardised at twenty-one throughout the Union, and trying to buy alcohol under age is not regarded as a youthful peccadillo, but as a serious offence. It is even illegal in many states to give anyone under the age of twenty-one a drink in a private house, at a party or even with a meal. There is more than an element of hysteria: in some states, bartenders who sell another drink to a drunk, who then goes out and drives his car into someone, can be held partially liable for the accident and sued by the victim. The same is true of a private person who allows his or her guests to drive home after one drink too many.

As already mentioned, it is illegal to drink in the street or in your car in most states, and theoretically illegal to have a bottle of wine with a picnic, though the last is enforced as capriciously as the 55mph speed limit. Furthermore, 'brown-bagging' (swigging from a bottle concealed in a brown paper bag) is not a particularly uncommon sight in the street: the brown bag satisfies the American sense of morality, which has always tended to be more concerned with what is seen to happen than with what actually happens – though in all fairness, the police may stop you if they see you doing it.

Despite this attitude towards liquor, or perhaps because of it (forbidden fruit, etc), parties are by no means unusual, though you will find that many people are drinking Perrier water or some unappetising soft drink or tooth-rotting non-alcoholic punch. What is worse, instead of cutting a slice of lime and putting it in the Perrier, which makes a delightful and refreshing drink that the most hardened drinker could still enjoy, they *buy* 'Perrier with a Twist', in which the citrus flavour has been added by the bottler; the result resembles unsweetened, uncoloured, but still synthetic-tasting orangeade.

This is as good a place as anywhere else to talk about meeting the opposite sex, though much of what has been said in Chapter 5 about making friends also applies. Bars are not particularly good meeting places, unless you like your sex casual, because most tend to be low-grade 'meat markets', but owing to the general openness and friendliness of Americans, it is seldom difficult to start a conversation anywhere, whether at a party or in a supermarket check-out line, and the Anglophilia of most Americans is such that the moment they hear your accent, they are likely to be more than willing to talk to you.

One thing which the more reserved Briton may find slightly surprising is the directness of most Americans in sexual matters, though this will depend on the circles in which he or she moves in Britain. Affaires often proceed at a rather more rapid rate than is usual in the Old World, and there is a greater tendency to talk about everything, rather than leaving it to chance and understanding. It can be very enlightening to listen to one of the many 'talk-radio' shows where a psychiatrist answers phone-in questions about love, sex and so forth, if you want an insight into American attitudes. As might be obvious from what has already been said about bars and restaurants, a meal rather than a drink is a typical 'first date', but it is important to agree upon a cuisine which suits you both; more than one promising encounter has foundered on raw fish!

Sexual *mores* do of course vary widely from place to place, and there is no doubt that even in the most freewheeling areas, notably California and New York city, the spread of herpes and latterly AIDS has discouraged the casual sex which was common in the sixties and seventies. Another point which is worth making is that there are still some truly astonishing ages of consent on the books in the United States: in many states, the age of consent is eighteen, which means that sleeping with a seventeen-year-old girlfriend can land a man in jail, not that it seems to stop most people. There is also the wonderful old Mann Act, which prohibits the transportation of women across state lines for immoral purposes, so a man cannot simply ship his girlfriend to a state where the age of consent is lower, unless he intends to marry her (see the section on marrying ages on page 55 (Chapter 5). As an interesting British legal aside, a British man may not be able to contract a valid marriage with a girl under the *British* age of consent, even though it is valid in the country in which it takes place!

As for 'substances', the attitude towards marijuana varies just as much in the United States as it does in the UK, and local enforcement attitudes vary equally widely. In California, possession of an amount of less than 1oz is a misdemeanour rather than a felony, and it is not an offence which is taken seriously (though felony possession is), but in some other states no distinction is made either as to quantity or as to the dangers of a drug; the penalties can be ferocious. Pills of various sorts (Dexedrine, etc), like the poor, have ye always with ye: penalties and attitudes are much as in the UK. Cocaine is apparently less popular than it was, though it may simply be that the media are paying less attention to it, but the penalties are stiff. Heroin is a small but serious problem, as in Britain. One big difference, though, is that whereas Britain is generally more concerned with trying to *help* drug users, many American states are more concerned with trying to *punish* them, and this is particularly true if you are caught trying to transport drugs across state lines.

Moving on to healthier preoccupations, there is the American attitude towards exercise. Those who take exercise in the United States are divided into two groups, one small and one large, though fortunately the small is constantly being swollen by defectors from the large. Exercise for the fun of it is only taken by the few; the rest latch onto whatever is fashionable, or the latest fad. Jogging was perhaps the first, and then more serious running replaced it. Tennis was always a fashionable game, and then it was supplanted by squash, and after that came racquets (whatever that is). Cycling enjoys a certain vogue, which seems to be on the increase. Aerobics and other gymnasium activities are also enjoying a boom, and if you are in the US only for a few months you may well be able to strike a deal with a local gymnasium, paying a proportion of the year's subscription for a short-term membership. A sport which enjoyed only a very brief vogue in the UK, but which flourishes in the United States and provides excellent opportunities for moderate and quite enjoyable exercise, is tenpin bowling: the only real drawbacks are the scoring, which is fiendishly complicated, and the danger of ricking your shoulder if you use the 16lb ball too fast and too often before you have become used to the game.

Swimming is of course very popular, not just in the Sunbelt (where private pools proliferate, and almost all condos provide a pool) but also in much of the rest of the country: even where winters are hard, summers are likely to be warmer than in Britain, and a pool can be very welcome. One slight surprise to ocean swimmers may be that the Pacific is astonishingly chilly. This is due to the cooling effect of the Humboldt current, the cold counterpart of the warm Gulf Stream which makes the Atlantic more tolerable.

In winter, skiing is a popular sport. There are downhill ski resorts in many areas, though they can become extremely crowded; ski-lift tickets actually have to be bought in advance in some popular resorts. On the other hand, cross-country skiing in the North and the high sierras provides a wonderful opportunity of seeing beautiful countryside in deserted splendour.

The golf course is as much a place for business meetings as for exercise in the United States, and the widespread habit of riding about in golf carts means that it often does not provide a tenth of the healthy exercise that it does in the UK. Among Yuppies, squash and racquets are also a business exercise.

'Country clubs' are similar to their English counterparts, social clubs with slightly sporting leanings, so that members can play tennis or golf or whatever, or simply sit in the bar. They are very much a business institution, and they are also rather male-dominated; all-male 'breakfast clubs' are by no means an unusual phenomenon, where American men gather to get away from their wives and to re-create the somewhat childish atmosphere of a fraternity house. There is a good deal of subdued rowdiness and coarse joking, mostly on a schoolboy level: a 'rude word' is a good way to get a laugh. In many ways, they are simply an upper-class (or at least, less working-class) version of the Moose Lodges, the Elks, and the other clubs to which many men belong in the US, and which are a bit like childhood 'gangs'. American men seem to have a tremendous weakness for these little boys' clubs, though sometimes it seems that this is mainly to annoy their wives and (in all fairness) to escape from the straitjacket which long business hours and short vacations place on the average American male.

There is no great tradition of amateur team sports for adults in the US – certainly nothing like British rugger and soccer clubs – though baseball and (to a very limited extent) football are played; on the other hand, out-of-school sports for children are rather more common, with Little League baseball the best known, and many adults are involved in this, as coaches and helpers.

Spectator sport is every bit as popular in the United States as in the UK, and soccer is increasing in popularity without, however, diminishing the power of baseball, basketball or American football one bit. For those unfamiliar with the rules of these sports, baseball is very much like the children's game of rounders (though more fun), basketball is similar to netball, and American football is *not* like rugby played by men in armour, but a bizarre game where the aim is not just to score goals but also to 'capture territory'. The pitch is marked out with lines at 10yd intervals, and if a team cannot gain 10yd within four 'plays' (a 'play' ends when the ball touches the ground or goes off at the side), the ball is given to the other side! This is only one of the surprising rules – others include the right to swap players between the team and the bench (something like reserves, who sit on the side) according to the coach's estimate of who will succeed best in a particular play, and the fact that some of the players actually on the field may be ineligible to catch the ball; this does not appear to be like the ban on passing forwards in rugger, but is altogether less comprehensible. The only reason for these few puzzled lines here is to show that if you want to follow the game, you are going to have to study it.

The Great Outdoors is another American archetype, and there can be no doubting that it is every bit as great as it is painted. Whenever we write about the American country-side, the difficulty lies in not over-writing and getting too enthusiastic, especially about the wonderful National Parks. Whether you just want a ten-minute constitutional or a week's hike in primeval wilderness, the American country-side can provide it. Of all that is good in America, the scenery is perhaps the best and the least exhaustible, whether you want the pastoral East or the majestic West.

Afficionados of motor sports will know the state of the game in the United States, but one particular variety of participatory sport which is worth mentioning is off-road and desert driving. Although this is (quite properly) banned in many areas, because of the way that trail bikes and four-wheel-drives can tear up local ecosystems, there are still plenty of places where you can get away from it all in a motor vehicle. Many Americans have expensive 'fun' off-road vehicles but, curiously, the most expensive (and often the most impressive looking) are the least effective. ATVs (All Terrain Vehicles, three- or four-wheeled motorcycles) are much less versatile and less fun than off-road motorcycles, but they are easier to learn to ride – though, unfortunately, this very ease of riding also makes it easier to get into trouble with them, and there is talk of banning them. Similarly, 'customised' American and Japanese four-wheel drives are usually much less effective off-road vehicles than their unmodified counterparts, and none can hold a candle to the humble Land-Rover, despite all their trick suspension, jacked bodies, and chromed lights and ornaments.

Among spectator motor sports, it is also worth mentioning that drag racing is very much more popular in the US than in the UK, and that stock-car races, which are also more common, are generally known as 'Demolition Derbys'.

13
Education

Education in the United States is an area in which differences in administration are fundamental, and differences in content are significant. Although this chapter is intended to be of use to parents, students and teachers, it is useful to begin with a basic appreciation of the system, then to go on and consider the student's point of view, and finally to go on to teaching.

Basically, the system is simple. Children first go to school at six, and then progress logically through twelve years or 'grades' until they finally come out at eighteen. In theory, a child may be required to repeat a grade if his or her accomplishments are not up to scratch, but this is very rare nowadays.

Unfortunately, within this admirably simple framework, the details are simply mind-boggling. First, we shall deal with the public system. In the United States, logically, schools which are open to the public at large free of charge are called 'public' schools, while fee-paying schools are called 'private' schools. Trying to explain to an American that in Britain, all public schools are private schools, while not all private schools are public schools, and that what they call public schools are called state schools, makes you realise that the British system has its illogicalities too. Then again, Americans use the word 'school' indiscriminately for schools, colleges and universities . . .

First of all, an additional grade or *kindergarten* has been grafted onto the front of the system. This corresponds to the British 'infants', and is often in a separate building from the next step, which is called *grade school*, and comprises six grades, from first to sixth. Grade school may however be further subdivided (and housed in two different buildings), to give *primary school* and *elementary school*. This grade-school period corresponds roughly to a British 'junior' or 'primary' school. Then, for the seventh grade (at the age of twelve) the child changes schools again and goes to a *junior high school*. At the end of the eighth grade, he or she changes schools again, to *senior high school*, or simply *high school* – unless the academic catchment area is not great, in which case junior and senior high schools are combined into one building. Then again, some junior high schools go through to ninth grade, with tenth, eleventh and twelfth grades as senior high.

Traditionally, the end of the twelfth grade was marked with a graduation ceremony; in order to graduate, you had to have satisfactory grades in all subjects (we shall return to this in a moment), and the effect was something like a matriculation or *baccalaureat*. Then, the end of junior high school was also marked by a 'graduation' – a substantially meaningless activity, but it did provide a bit of a ceremony for the academically less able, as most people manage to complete eighth (or ninth) grade satisfactorily. Not to be outdone, grade schools then introduced 'graduation', and now even kindergartens hold them!

To make life more confusing, 'grades' are not just academic years; they are also the way in which a child's progress is measured. These appear simple enough – from A to D – and represent the spectrum from 'very good' (A), through 'average' (C) to 'poor' (D); an unmitigated fail is an F. Often, these grades are embellished with pluses or minuses, but the fundamental point is that they are all *internal* or comparative grades, and depend very much on the general standard of the school: there is no external assessment system along the lines of the British 'O' and 'A' levels, and grades cannot even realistically be compared with CSEs, as they are based almost entirely on course-work and regular small tests rather than having a substantial examination element.

This is one of the places where states differ enormously. Not only do standards vary greatly from school to school, but also from state to state and from time to time. Some states attempt to impose some sort of uniformity – the old New York State Regent's Exam was very much like a British GCE – but others make no attempt either to impose or even to measure standards. In the late 1960s and throughout most of the 1970s, California's public school system was a byword for uselessness, where children acquired an education despite their environment, rather than because of it, but towards the end of the 1970s they began to improve again, and at the time of writing they were apparently at least as good as the national average (which is not saying much).

The range of subjects taught also varies; the habit of lumping geography and history together as 'humanities' originated in the United States, as did many other developments (unwelcome in the view of the authors) in British education, such as 'team teaching', 'mixed-ability teaching', and the invention of such vague subjects as 'related studies' or 'civics'. It is true that many things which look like anarchy to an outsider do make sense in a professional teaching context, and that it is as absurd to expect schools to be the way they were thirty years ago as to accept every passing academic fad. Nevertheless, it is advisable to examine any school to which you propose to send your children with considerable care.

As well as differing in academic organisation, American public schools are different from the UK in a number of other ways, too. They are usually very large – a typical graduating year might range from a hundred in a small school to a thousand in a major school in a big city – and they are severely over-administered, in the sense that 'administrative' staff sometimes begin to rival academic staff in numbers: there are administrators for the school, for the years, and for 'guidance' (careers). There is rarely an assembly in the morning – the whole school may only meet once a week or even once a month – and the affairs which are traditionally dealt with in a British school assembly are dealt with in 'Home Room', the equivalent of a form. There is never a 'house' system in the British pattern, and sports are not accorded half the importance *in the curriculum* which they are in the UK: most sport is extracurricular, though some is subsumed into PE classes, with ad hoc teams being picked from the class. Sport is regarded as the province of 'jocks', the children who are really keen and who often let sport get in the way of their academic work.

There is never a school uniform, and discipline in general is very slack. In inner-city schools, depths are plumbed which are undreamt of in Britain: senior children deal in drugs, and arguments are settled with knives or even guns. One friend of the authors was given police protection at school because the local drug king (a boy of the same age) took exception to him; another, who was a teacher, suffered a nervous breakdown which her psychiatrist described as resembling battle fatigue in Vietnam veterans, though she was arguably luckier than one of her colleagues at the same school, who was thrown out of a first-storey window by a disaffected pupil.

From all this, it is obvious that children who have passed through twelve years of the American school system are unlikely to be either as knowledgeable or as academically (or otherwise) disciplined as their British counterparts: even if the schools were as good, which in most cases they are not, the children will have had a couple of years less education than if they had been through the English 'mill' and taken 'A' levels.

This is reflected in the American university system, which in many ways is simply a continuation of the school system. It is not unrealistic to say that the first couple of years at an American university correspond to English 'A' levels, though the degree of specialisation is still nothing like as great, and subjects are taught which any British undergraduate would be expected to have mastered at school: science undergraduates, for example, are required to take English and history courses.

The next couple of years (American degree courses typically last four years) sees a growth in 'electives', where the student seriously begins to study his or her chosen subject: these probably correspond to the first year or year and a half of a regular British university course.

Because there are virtually no entrance requirements for many of the public universities, and given the very low level of first-degree work, it is little surprise that college degrees are much more common in the United States than in Britain; nor is it any surprise that many people take master's degrees, which are primarily by course-work, and which seem to British eyes no more than finishing off your first degree. This is not strictly a fair appraisal, though, as an MA or MSc typically takes *another* three years, which puts the American MA and MSc rather ahead of the British BA and BSc, and makes it roughly comparable with a British master's degree by coursework. As a matter of interest, an LLB is always a postgraduate degree in the United States.

As with schools, academic differences are not the only ones. Not all universities operate three terms a year: some have four terms, and some only two. Furthermore, they are operated on a 'cafeteria' system: various courses are offered (in the 'college catalogue' issued each year by each university), and the students select whatever they wish. Each course brings a number of 'credits' and when you have amassed enough credits, you get a degree – though you must also have passed certain required courses, rather than obtaining just any credits, which is why it is possible to spend several academically profitable years at university and still fail to graduate, simply because you missed out on a vital 'requirement' in, say, freshman English!

Even when you do graduate (or as the Americans say, 'are graduated'), the way in which the degrees are 'scored' is different from the British system. As in school, your degree depends upon your grade average more than on your examination prowess; 'finals', to an American, are examinations taken at the end of each *course*, rather than at the end of the final year, and as a course lasts a term, an American student can take a large number of 'finals'. Then, instead of being awarded a First, an Upper or Lower Second, or whatever, he or she is awarded simply a degree, with no mention of 'Hons' or 'Pass'. The very top students will be described as having graduated *summa cum laude*, and those who are only a little lower as *magna cum laude*, while any who are generally felt to have done well and who have maintained a high grade average may be mentioned on the 'Dean's List'.

There is no charge for tuition in public schools or universities, though free university education is only available to residents of the state in which the university is situated, and there may be nominal registration and per-term fees; going to an out-of-state university means that you have to pay an economic rate. The only requirements are residence, however, and it does not matter if the student's parents are not American. At least, that is the case in most places, but with American isolationism once again on the increase, and ever-growing pressure from taxpayers to cut public expenditure, this may change.

On the other hand, there are no grants either – and you have to live while you are at university. If your parents pay, all well and good, but there is also a long-established tradition of 'working your way through college', taking part-time jobs and working all through the (very long) summer vacation to support yourself. Various systems of student loans have been tried, but the drawback, from the government's point of view, was that many people simply did not bother to pay back the loans; they are currently being encouraged to do so by the IRS, which withholds tax over-payments due back to them until they pay up.

In addition to the universities, there are also 'community colleges' or 'junior colleges', which award an Associate degree after only two years' study; these degrees are roughly equivalent to an English Higher National Diploma (HND), and are called AAs – Associate of Arts, not Alcoholics Anony-mous, though there are schools which offer courses in bartending. In fact, there are trade schools of all types, which award either their own diplomas ('Certificates of Completion') or AA degrees, usually after two years' study again.

Finally, there are also colleges which are accredited by the state and have the right to award bachelor's degrees, but do not have the status of universities; their nearest equivalent in Britain is probably the 'Poly' or the college of further education.

So much for the public system. As in Britain (and perhaps with even greater justification), there is a flourishing parallel system of private education and, unlike Britain, which only has one genuinely private university, almost all the better universities in the United States are private.

Within the American school system, it is possible to find the equivalent of pretty much any school in the English system, plus a few more variants, but the equivalents are not always exact. For example, most Americans would say that the nearest thing to a traditional British public school was a 'military academy', but many of these places make the harshest British schools seem like a holiday camp. In most, the children actually wear a military-style uniform and are subject to military-style discipline, haircuts and punish-ments; the authors' view is that most children find school bad enough without all this, and it is hard to see what kind of person sends their children there. Admittedly they are less popular than they were, but they still exist, and are much favoured by some for 'problem children', though it can be argued that the 'problem' in this case might be self-fulfilling and self-perpetuating.

A rather closer parallel to a British public school is what the Americans call a 'preparatory' school, though in trans-atlantic usage the 'preparation' is for university (usually the

Ivy League) rather than for a public school (which the Americans call a private school), so the scope for confusion in this area alone is considerable. It does, however, explain the American usage of 'preppy' to describe Hooray Henry and Sloane Ranger types. American 'prep' schools flourish on the East Coast, are almost unheard-of on the West Coast, and are hotbeds of snobbery. Prep schools are mostly (but far from all) single-sex.

In practice, the major alternatives to public schools in the United States are usually run by religious orders, and vary from something resembling an English Catholic public school, through convent schools of varying degrees of repressiveness to hotbeds of tub-thumping religious extremism usually associated with the more fundamentalist sects; religion may not, of course, be taught in public schools. In the US, the term 'parochial' school is normally used to describe all church-run schools; unlike the UK, the term implies neither a primary school nor a small local school of no special interest. It is as well to investigate any religious school fairly thoroughly, to make sure that they correspond both to your own beliefs and to the extent to which you wish to have your children force-fed religion.

Although parochial and prep schools are the main choices in the private system, there are also 'progressive' schools on the Dartington or even Summerhill model; schools where sport is paramount; schools for other special abilities, such as art, drama and dance (*vide Fame*); and private schools catering to children with learning or physical disabilities of various kinds.

As for universities, it is as important as in Britain to distinguish between the ones with *social* status and the *academically* significant ones. For example, the Massachusetts Institute of Technology and the California Institute of Technology are academically world-class, but socially rather dubious: they are seen as a refuge for 'science nerds' and misfits, simply because of their academic excellence. The 'Ivy League' and the 'Heavenly Seven', which were traditionally the leading universities, men's and women's respectively, are socially impeccable, but academically patchier; the Harvard Law School is justifiably world-famous, but in the popular mind both Yale and Princeton are better known for football than for anything else. Both the Ivy League and the Heavenly Seven (which includes universities such as Vassar and Smith) are now mostly co-educational.

Apart from the really well-known universities, it is very much a question of investigating the local institutions, and trying to gauge their reputation by talking to people, looking at who is on the faculty, and reading the catalogues (prospectus). In Los Angeles, for instance, USC (the University of Southern California, also known as the University of Spoiled Children) has a certain social cachet, and is academically strong in several areas; but if you wanted to read Law, you would be better at Loyola, and for theatre, the state-run CSULB (California State University at Long Beach) is hard to beat, though some would argue for UCLA's primacy. There are actually two state universities, Cal State and the University of California, and both have branches throughout the state; the well-known UCLA is the University of California at Los Angeles.

There are also various *private* trade schools and junior colleges, similar to those described in the public sector. Again in Los Angeles, there is a highly regarded fashion school for would-be clothes designers.

By now, the implications for students will be clear. Life at school is different from that in Britain, both academically and socially, and although academically it is likely to be less promising, socially it is probably more interesting. Life at university is a very different matter. Financially it will be a burden, even if tuition is free, or almost free, because there is no grant. Academically, it is going to be a very slow way of reaching the kind of standard which a British university expects in three years. Socially, it may be interesting, but the restrictions on drinking noted in the last chapter may prove very tiresome to British students, used to drinking legally from the age of eighteen and (usually) illegally from sixteen or seventeen. Many American university students find it almost impossible to believe that British university unions always have bars, and that drinking is legal; certainly, American students drink, but they do so both illegally and in contravention of college regulations. Like many American laws, enforcement is capricious, but American students do face suspension and even being sent down if they are discovered.

It is probably a mistake, therefore, to think of an American undergraduate course as a serious alternative to British university, at least after 'A' levels. For postgraduate research, on the other hand, they can be an excellent idea, and an option which is worth considering is going on to an American BA course after 'O' levels; one of the authors was offered a place at one of the better state universities at the age of sixteen, on the strength of nine 'O' levels, and if he had been able to take the offer up, he would only have been a year younger than his contemporaries and probably academically better qualified. As it was, both cost and his own timidity ruled it out, but a BA at twenty would still have allowed him to take his LLB at only a year or two older than he finally did, and to have had a broader education into the bargain.

One last way in which American universities differ significantly from British ones is the existence of 'fraternities', 'sororities', and 'honor societies', and although most British people have a vague idea of what these are (especially if they have seen National Lampoon's *Animal House* film), they are worth a little more explanation.

Fraternities and sororities are basically social clubs. They are named by meaningless triads of Greek letters, which are worn on 'pins'; for a boy to give his fraternity pin to a girl is regarded as half-way to an engagement. Both fraternities and sororities maintain private halls of residence, known as 'fraternity houses' or 'sorority houses', and these are used for entertaining both by members who live there and by those who live elsewhere. Membership of fraternities and sororities is regarded as a major social achievement by some people, and as a childish irrelevance by others; both viewpoints are easily justified. At the beginning of each year, new students ('freshmen' or 'froshes') are wooed or 'rushed' by the fraternities or sororities, who make their own judgement of the newcomers' social worth, and make their pitch accordingly. Both fraternities and sororities exist independently of the universities, and may indeed be national; a member of, say, Sigma Chi fraternity is welcomed by other Sigma Chi fraternities all over the United States (this particular fraternity is so well known by its first two letters that everyone forgets the third).

'Honor' societies are rather different, though some still use Greek letters; the authors have often thought of making up a Phi Upsilon Kappa pin, but as few Americans read Greek, the joke would be lost. Entry to an 'honor' society is dependent on academic ability (as measured by grade averages) and they function partly as social clubs and partly as information and 'old boy' (or 'old girl') networks in later life – though fraternities and sororities do the same to a certain extent. They do not maintain 'houses' and are altogether more sober institutions.

Finally, from a teacher's point of view, a great deal depends on the level at which you wish to teach and upon the state requirements in the place where you are going. If you are in the realms where a British university chair is in sight, American chairs are obviously also achievable, though it is worth noting that the term 'professor' is thrown around a good deal more casually in the US than in the UK; there are also 'associate professors' and 'assistant professors', and often these correspond simply to 'lecturer' (or even 'reader') in the British system. If you go for a year or two, on an expressly temporary basis, you will usually be accorded the title of 'Visiting Professor', which looks good on the curriculum vitae.

At high school and grade level recruiting is at county or even town level, so the only practical approach is to go to one of the organisations which specialises in teacher exchanges or visits. Reciprocal accreditation requirements should be possible with most states, unless you do not have a degree, but you will obviously need to check individual cases.

14
Staying On

Although this is not designed primarily as a handbook for permanent immigrants to the United States, there will no doubt be some among our readers who will at least wish to consider staying on, and some who will actually do so. In this context, 'staying on' means making the decision to make the United States your permanent home, though you may always have it at the back of your mind to return to the UK at some more-or-less distant point in the future.

Quite apart from the career aspects of the decision, which only you can make, you will need to consider the following. First, your legal (immigrant) status in the US, which is covered in Chapter 6. Secondly, your family's reaction, and their prospects. Thirdly, the prospects for your own old age, and for health care. Finally, the possibility of taking out US citizenship.

Unless you already have a Green Card entitling you to immigrant status, you will need to get one. As already explained, if you have married a US citizen (a common reason for deciding to stay in the US), this is time-consuming and annoying, but not too difficult. Otherwise, you will need to persuade either your present employer or a prospective employer to help you to get one, and the ease with which you can do this will depend very much on your relationship with your employer (or prospective employer) and on your own skills and abilities. Most reasonably senior managers, or anyone else with special skills which their employers value highly, can get a Green Card fairly easily, though if you are planning on changing jobs and your future employer is trying to get you a Green Card, it is as well (for obvious reasons) to conceal the fact both from your present employer and from the Immigration Service, at least until the application is made.

The family's reaction is a subject which has probably been canvassed enough in this book already, but an important point is their employment prospects, as well as the prospects of your children staying in the country; remember that on most non-immigrant visas, children cease to be included on the parents' visa (or to be eligible for their own visas on the strength of the parents' visas, if they have passports of their own) as soon as they marry or reach twenty-one, whichever is sooner – although, of course, if they marry US citizens the position will be rather different. Otherwise, they will be accorded preferential immigrant status (see Chapter 6 again), but it can still take a very long time for them to gain immigrant visas in their own right. On the other hand, if you have an immigrant visa, your children will be allowed to work legally as long as they can stay in the country legally.

If your children were born in the US, they will usually be eligible for US citizenship, in which case their children will be American citizens; on the other hand, although your children may retain their British citizenship even if they were born in the US, your grandchildren may have some difficulty in claiming British citizenship if they, too, are born in the US. Individual cases vary, but the tendency of British immigration law is to become more and more exclusive, and who can tell what may happen in twenty or thirty years' time?

The prospects for your old age are really much the same as they are in the UK, except for two things. The statutory pension is slightly more generous if you have contributed all your life (and you must in any case contribute for a minimum of forty quarter-years), but it is still far from lavish. Secondly, the age at which it is payable is scheduled to *rise* steadily, which accurately reflects the extended active life of the typical person nowadays, but which unfortunately takes no account of the ever-decreasing age of retirement: to be brutal, what do you live on between retiring from your initial job, and getting a pension? It is also worth reflecting upon the fact that the American Social Security system was, at least in the mid-1980s, looking extremely shaky; the high-water mark of benefits had probably passed, as in most countries in the world, and more money was flowing out than could be brought in by any reasonable (or politically acceptable) increase in taxation.

In practice, either a firm's pension or an IRA (Individual Retirement Account) is going to be as essential in the US as in the UK if you want to supplement your statutory pension, and there is really no advice that is applicable in the US which is not also applicable in the UK, except that the tax penalties for closing an IRA before the contracted term may be worse in the US. As in the UK, permitted percentages of income which may be contributed, and the most tax-efficient way of contributing, will vary periodically – almost from year to year – and there is no substitute for the advice of a good accountant. The same is true for other forms of tax-sheltered savings and (once again) it is worth emphasising that American rules tend to be a good deal stricter than British ones.

What has already been said about medical insurance does not need repeating, but it is worth adding that if you or any of your family contracts a very serious, expensive or chronic disease, you can find yourself running out of insurance unless you are very careful, and paying truly alarming bills even if you remain insured. It is well worth checking whether your firm's pension also carries any form of supplementary insurance to back up Medicare – and what happens before you are eligible for Medicare. A common ploy is to latch onto the policy provided by a good employer, and then stick with it after you have left him, even if it means doing so at your own expense.

If you have a Green Card, there is no particular advantage to obtaining US citizenship unless you want to vote or to stand for election (and, in any case, you will be unable to stand for President because you will not be an American-born citizen).

In addition, it is now impossible under American law to hold dual nationality (though it used to be possible). This is less of a problem than it may seem, because dual nationality is perfectly possible under *British* law, and the fact that the Americans don't like it does not affect Her Majesty's Government. Once again, law on this can change, especially if your dual nationality involves taking oaths of allegiance to a foreign power (which taking out American citizenship certainly will), so it is worth checking in detail whether it is worth while for you personally, or for your family. An important factor if military conscription is re-introduced in the United States (it is currently in abeyance) is that while Green Card holders are liable for the draft, they may also legitimately leave the country; citizens will not legally have this option. Should you decide to go for citizenship, it is as well to engage an American immigration lawyer; these are not difficult to find, and are usually listed in the Yellow Pages in most major American cities.

15
Going Home

For many people, the decision to go home is very nearly as difficult as the original decision to go, or to stay on. It is always tempting to stick with what you know, and if you have been living and working in the United States, you may find that the UK has changed more than you think. A particular example may be a change of government: if a party which is not to your liking is in power in Britain, the adjustment to returning home will be that much more difficult.

Although the career advantages of time spent in the United States are obvious in the abstract, they are rather less clear when you start considering concrete examples. If you are simply on a foreign posting, and you will still be working for the same firm when you get home, the question is less pressing; if you feel that there will be an advantage in changing jobs when you get home, you can worry about that when you get there. But if your contract in the United States is about to expire, or if you feel that you have learned all that you can usefully learn before making your next move, and you are going to resign from your present position, matters are rather less clear cut.

Obviously, a great deal will depend on your position. If you are high enough up the totem pole, it is usually only a question of letting it be known that you are available, and perhaps of talking to a few international or London-based 'head-hunters'; you may also wish to consider the possibility of living and working in yet a third country, in which case one of the other guides in this series may be able to help you. If you are not in quite such an exalted position, reading the 'sits vac' columns in British papers is an obvious approach. If you see something that interests you, even if the closing date for applications means that you are unlikely to be in the UK, a letter stating your interest and the date of your return may well pique a prospective employer's interest. If at the very worst you have no serious leads when your time is up, you will need to reconcile yourself to living off your savings for a while until you find a job, which can be an alarming prospect.

In making the decision to return, you will of course need to consider all the things which have already been covered in this book, including paperwork, transportation, accommodation in the UK, the kind of lifestyle you can expect when you return, and your family's feelings and needs as well as your own job prospects. The 'grass is greener' syndrome is always one to beware of, as is homesickness for one place or the other; more than one friend of the authors has spent literally thousands of pounds shuttling between the two countries, moving more because of shortcomings (or imagined shortcomings) in the place where they found themselves, or because of equally illusory advantages on the other side of the Atlantic, than on any rational basis. In one case (that of an unmarried electronics engineer), the experience he gained enabled him to set up as a successful consultant in the UK; in the other, where there was a man, a non-working wife, and a teenage daughter, the family was nearly financially ruined.

Taking paperwork, transportation, accommodation, lifestyle and family needs in order, the least troubling is usually paperwork. You will need to satisfy the IRS that you do not owe Uncle Sam any money, and if you have been abroad for more than three years you will need to re-establish yourself in the British National Insurance system, but this is not difficult: your employer will do it for you, or your accountant if you are self-employed.

You will have rather more fun if you have meanwhile married a US citizen, or had any children, though British immigration is a good deal less difficult about wives and children than US immigration. The procedure is explained in a leaflet obtainable from the Home Office Immigration and Nationality Department, Lunar House, Wellesley Road, Croydon, Surrey, but the easiest way to do it is to get your spouse in on a tourist visa (six months) and then to take your marriage certificate along to immigration headquarters in Croydon: your spouse fills in a brief declaration, and he or she is issued with a letter purporting to be from the Home Secretary, stating that he or she has right of residence in the UK. A stamp to that effect will also be entered in his or her passport and automatically renewed (on production of the letter or the old passport) when the passport is renewed. The main hurdle lies in getting your spouse into the UK in the first place. A six-month visitor visa is usually easy enough, but in strict theory, you are supposed to sort all this out beforehand with the British Embassy or Consulate in the country in which you are living. Embassies are normally reasonably helpful, but slow; Consulates are much more variable, and when we returned to the UK together for the first time, the woman at the Los Angeles consulate was so rude and indeed obstructive – a Jill-in-office, if that is the feminine of Jack-in-office – that we decided to do it via the visitor visa, which is a bit of a risk. The best thing to do is to get HMSO publications HC 169 and HC 503, which explain the rules in some detail.

If you have an American fiancé or fiancée, the procedure is even more of a business, as a 'fiancé(e) visa' is only good for three months instead of the usual six – the very opposite of what you would expect – and you are required to provide proof (in the form of a letter from the church minister, or a registry office booking and a letter from the registrar) that the wedding will take place within three months. Unless you can do this, it is usually easier to go for a visitor's visa again.

If you are on a foreign posting with your company or organisation, your return fare will normally be paid (though they may place limits on transporting your household goods, and some may even be awkward about paying for family members acquired in the United States). Otherwise, you are letting yourself in for a stiff expenditure. Customs on your return to the UK is normally very relaxed, and they do not require anything like the detailed inventories that the American customs service do. On the other hand, it is important to be absolutely honest with them: their discretionary powers are wide, and if you try to take advantage of their easygoing approach, they may well decide to tax everything in sight. The general rule is that if you have had possession and use of goods for six months in the preceding twelve, they are regarded as personal effects and are imported free of duty; in practice, items less than six months old will also be waved through, unless you have bought a lot of expensive new toys (such as cameras, portable music centres etc) in the last few months. It is also important to read the list of prohibited and restricted items carefully: British customs take a dim view of tear-gas canisters, and pets will of course have to be quarantined. For cats and dogs, the period is six months, and although no visiting is allowed for the first fourteen days (by Ministry of Agriculture regulations), you can visit your pet *in his or her locked quarters* after that – though visiting hours may vary. Quarantine is expensive; the price in late 1985 was typically £500–600 per animal for the entire period, or (say) the price of three weeks in a decent London hotel for their owners.

Again, accommodation is merely a practical matter, but if you have let your house you would be well advised to give your tenants plenty of notice and to get reassurance from your agent or solicitor that your house will in fact be available when you get back. Otherwise, observations about finding somewhere to live in the UK are much as they are for finding somewhere to live in the US.

Lifestyle is another matter. Whenever you have been living abroad for a while, there are always things at home which assume enormous proportions in your mind, things which are unavailable where you have been living. Ben Gunn, in *Treasure Island*, tells young Jim 'Many's the night I've dreamed of cheese – toasted, mostly.' In India, you dream of a thick, juicy steak, a piece of good beef served rare. In America, you may think wistfully of a pint of warm, flat, strong beer, Marston's Owd Rodger perhaps, or of a loaf of really good bread.

The truth though is that once you have had your cheese, or your steak, or your beer, or your bread, you soon realise that there are a lot of things which you miss about the place you have just come from. It may seem quite medieval, for instance, to have to go to half a dozen different shops to buy food, instead of stopping at the supermarket – and it is likely to be very annoying indeed when you realise that these shops either close ridiculously early, or carry a very limited range of goods and charge inflated prices for them in return for staying open 'late' (such as to 7pm or 8pm.) Admittedly, there are a few twenty-four shops in London, but what has been said about limited stocks and soaring prices applies all the more strongly to them. For all that has been said about America's anti-liquor feeling, it will also come as a shock to pay about twice as much for a bottle of spirits; and if you wear blue jeans, paying 50 per cent more for a pair of Levi's is not much fun, either. The price of petrol will really horrify you.

You will miss the restaurants and the habit of eating out; you will of course miss your American friends, though you may have old friendships in the UK that you can pick up without effort. The lackadaisical attitude of British shop assistants will drive you up the wall; anyone who ignored the customers as studiously as many British shop assistants would be out on their ear in a matter of days in an American store.

If you have been living in the Sunbelt (and in the authors' opinion, anyone who has the opportunity should), you will miss the weather; it is a distressing thought that London is on the same latitude as Edmonton, Alberta. If you enjoy skiing, you will also miss that, or at least easy access to it.

Your real income is likely to be significantly lower, too, though this will (as already mentioned) depend very much on both the kind of work that you do and on how you like to spend your money. Obviously, figures will change with inflation, and the 'rule of two' can be applied to convert these sums to British income, but at the time of writing it seemed that anyone with a very low income (up to, say, $8,000–10,000 a year) was worse off in the United States; that anyone in the moderate range, from $10,000 to somewhere around $25–35,000, was considerably better off, with the differential relative to the UK increasing in direct proportion to their salary; and that above, say, $50,000 there was very little difference. The range from (about) $30,000 to $50,000 was, however, anomalous. Up to the lower range, most people buy domestically produced goods and live very well, but at between $25,000 and $35,000, they begin to buy imports, which makes the prices they pay soar, so that the moderately well-to-do person suddenly finds that his or her resources are strained if he or she wants to keep up with the local Joneses at the same income level.

Of course, money isn't everything. In the UK, you will be going back to probably *twice* as much annual holiday, and a generally much more relaxed attitude towards timekeeping, and if this is more important to you than money, you will be a lot happier; if you value European travel, this is another bonus.

If you have a family, though, there is the problem that they may not view things with the same equanimity. At the risk of sounding like a male chauvinist, it is in our experience depressingly usual for a man to take his wife to the US with him, more or less against her will, where she then spends her whole time complaining about the country and saying how beastly it is, all the while getting used to a high standard of living and to the undoubted conveniences of the American way of life. When the time comes to go home, her feelings are divided; when she gets home, she realises what she has lost, and rails against Britain as bitterly as she used to rail against America. It can happen, and it does. Something similar can arise if you marry in the US; nothing can be worse than to have your spouse constantly sniping at everything in the UK when you come back, as if it were your personal fault that the shops close on Sundays, there is never anywhere to park the car, and that you can't get a drink in a pub at four o'clock in the afternoon, just when you need one after a long walk in the country.

Although this is mainly a personal problem, it is compounded if your spouse works: it is rarely possible to synchronise resignations, let alone to do so at a point where the careers of both parties are equally advanced by the move. Planning well in advance is *essential*.

There may also be the question of the children's response. Small children – up to ten or twelve – are very adaptable, and regard moving about and losing friends with a fair degree of fatalism, but teenagers can become very antagonistic indeed. Parents may find it easier to understand if they can remember the troubles of their own teenage years, establishing friends and position, and the dread with which they might then have viewed being forced to do the same all over again. Teenage love affairs, too, may not seem so important from a perspective of twenty or thirty years on; but at the time, their intensity is (literally) unbelievable, and a forced separation can assume the proportions of grand opera.

On a more practical level, the children's schooling can be very important. It is widely believed by Americans as well as Britons that American education is inferior to British, and while this may not always be true (though its accuracy will vary from state to state), there is not much doubt that a child transferring from an American school to a British one will be at a greater disadvantage, especially in the teenage years, than one who transfers the other way. As with leaving Britain, the departure should be timed to coincide with a natural break – at the very least, the end of a school year, and preferably the transfer from one school to another (grade school to Junior High, Junior High to High, or even High School Graduation).

If the children are of university age, the problems are still greater. An American high school graduate is unlikely to possess anything like the degree of specialised knowledge which is expected of a new undergraduate at a British university or college, and the best solution may be a year or two at a British technical college or college of further education, taking 'A' levels, as a preparation for university. This can benefit the child in many ways, as it provides a useful half-way house between the controlled social and educational environment of school and the freer environment of self-directed study, while the American experience should provide a wider basis of experience and judgement on which to build educational achievement.

Although throughout the book we have tried to stress both advantages and disadvantages equally (because optimists always overlook the disadvantages, and pessimists always overlook the advantages), it is obviously essential from a personal point of view to concentrate on the advantages, and to make the best of where you are. Take responsibility for your decisions: stick to them, because you cannot blame anyone else for taking them for you. By all means travel, and return, and enjoy it, but remember the old Arab saying: 'Take what you want, and pay for it, saith the Lord'.

Appendix 1
Compendium

In this section, the bare geographical facts about the various states are given, together with a brief appreciation of each state. For convenience, they are grouped together by geographical proximity, though not in quite the same order as described in Chapter 1. This is because the unifying factor in this chapter is mainly climatic, rather than cultural. Populations are rounded very roughly, to the nearest quarter or even half million; this is because it is more useful in a book like this, which must stay in print for some years, to give a good general idea of the numbers rather than giving precise but out-of-date figures.

After a brief introduction to each area, the states are listed individually, together with their state capital, area, population, and a list of neighbouring states, which begins with the state to the north or north-east and continues clockwise.

NEW ENGLAND AND THE NORTH WEST

(Connecticut, Indiana, Maine, Massachusetts, Michigan, New Hampshire, New York, Ohio, Pennsylvania, Rhode Island, Vermont, West Virginia)

This is basically the north-eastern quarter of the United States. The New England climate typically comprises cold winters and mild summers; the central New England states are mostly below freezing from December to March, with typical July/August temperatures in the low-to-mid 70s Fahrenheit (20s Centigrade). The northern states are somewhat colder (Maine winters are legendary) and the southern states warmer; the seaboard states are wetter than the inland ones, though overall rainfall is comparable with the British Isles.

There are also greater extremes of temperature as you get further from the Atlantic: upstate New York, for example, is typically 15°F (8°C) warmer in summer, and 15°F (8°C) colder in winter, than Connecticut, and the same is true of the other states which border on the Great Lakes.

The landscape in this area is in many ways the most European in the United States, though population densities are much lower.

Appendix 1: Compendium

The states which make up 'New England' are marked with an asterisk. The farming land is more marginal than that further west, and some farms have even been abandoned because they are uneconomic. A common fate of farms around the major cities is 'gentrification' as a second home; the farmland will then either be allowed to return to its natural state, or be lightly managed as a hobby.

Formerly the main industrial area of the United States, New England proper has steadily lost ground to the central Atlantic states and to the other states of the north-east, though a number of 'sunrise' industries (particularly electronics) have relocated or been founded there.

Connecticut*
State capital Hartford
Area 5,000 square miles
Population 3,000,000
Neighbouring states Massachusetts, Rhode Island, New York

A typical New England state. Still surprisingly rural in many areas, with three-quarters of the state still wooded or forested, but with a variety of industries (mostly light, except shipbuilding), especially in defence and other federal areas of expenditure – Connecticut is third only to California and New York in this area, albeit a poor third. Diversified farming, including cattle-raising and tobacco. A favoured area for wealthy commuters into New York City.

Indiana
State capital Indianapolis
Area 36,290 square miles
Population 5,500,000
Neighbouring states Michigan, Ohio, Kentucky, Illinois

Indiana's state motto is 'The Crossroads of America', which was fair enough in the nineteenth century, but which now looks a bit grandiloquent in the light of the shift of industry to the Sunbelt. The richer farms are to the north, the poorer to the south, and although the area is traditionally described as the 'corn belt', much of the corn goes on feeding cattle, and soybean planting is about two-thirds as common as corn. Typical north-eastern mix of agriculture and industry, but less industrial than (say) Michigan.

Maine*
State capital Augusta
Area 33,220 square miles
Population 1,000,000
Neighbouring states New Hampshire (also borders Canada)

A cold, northern, sparsely-populated state which bulges up into Canada. Farming (dairy and latterly poultry, plus potatoes) and fishing are the traditional industries, now supplemented with summer tourism. Some light industry (mostly metal-working) in the south.

Massachusetts*
State capital Boston
Area 8,250 square miles
Population 6,000,000
Neighbouring states New Hampshire, Rhode Island, Connecticut, New York, Vermont

Full of history – the Revolution effectively started here – with a good deal of commerce, banking, etc. Popularly (and with some justification) regarded as the home of snobbery in America, but very friendly towards Britons. Much attractive scenery, in a pastoral mode. A surprising amount of (mostly light) industry, centred around Boston.

Michigan
State capital Lansing
Area 58,200 square miles
Population 9,000,000
Neighbouring states Ohio, Indiana, Wisconsin (also borders Canada and is a Great Lakes state)

Famous chiefly for industry – Detroit is in Michigan, along with much other heavy and light industry – but also (as usual) with a good deal of agriculture and wilderness in between. The industry followed the mining; both coal and iron ores exist, in huge quantities, in Michigan. Bitter winters.

New Hampshire*
State capital Concord
Area 9,300 square miles
Population 1,000,000
Neighbouring states Maine, Massachusetts, Vermont (also borders Canada)

Again, archetypally New England. Predominantly rural and agricultural, with some industry, mostly light. Increasing electronics and similar 'sunrise' involvement. A small sea-coast.

New York
State capital Albany
Area 49,500 square miles
Population 17,500,000
Neighbouring states Vermont, Massachusetts, Connecticut, New Jersey, Pennsylvania (also borders Canada)

Not just the home of The Big Apple, a city you either love or hate (few are indifferent), but also a very large state (it stretches to Lake Ontario) with several other major cities and a great deal of beautiful countryside. New York City is tucked away at the very bottom right of New York State. Industry of all kinds, and very varied agriculture – mostly hard fruit, but also others including grapes and wine.

Ohio
State capital Columbus
Area 41,100 square miles
Population 11,000,000
Neighbouring states Pennsylvania, West Virginia, Kentucky, Indiana, Michigan. (Coastline with Lake Erie)

A sometimes uneasy mix of mining, lumber, industry, and agriculture. Like Michigan, something of a 'sunset' state, with broken-down farms and declining industries in many areas, but still with much attractive countryside and some wilderness.

Pennsylvania
State capital Harrisburg
Area 45,300 square miles
Population 12,000,000
Neighbouring states New York, New Jersey, Delaware, Maryland, West Virginia, Ohio. (Coastline with Lake Erie)

Although not regarded as a New England state, has many New England characteristics, including a rather joyless outlook on life. On the other hand, plenty of ugly industry (Philadelphia, Pittsburgh) interspersed among the attractive countryside and some attractive towns. Noted for the Amish and for 'Pennsylvania Dutch' – actually *Deutsch*, German – settlers.

Rhode Island*
State capital Providence
Area 1,200 square miles
Population 1,000,000
Neighbouring states Massachusetts, Connecticut

America's smallest state. Much eighteenth- and nineteenth-century building; formerly *the* place for the 'cottages' (ie mansions) of nineteenth-century tycoons. Rural inland; traditionally fishing on the coast; a surprising amount of light industry; much tourism.

Vermont*
State capital Montpelier
Area 9,600 square miles
Population 500,000
Neighbouring states New Hampshire, Massachusetts, New York (also borders Canada)

Extremely rural; only one city (Burlington) exceeds 25,000 people. Typical modern New England mix of agriculture and tourism, though the south-west is attracting some 'sunrise' industries.

West Virginia
State capital Charleston
Area 24,180 square miles
Population 2,000,000
Neighbouring states Pennsylvania, Maryland, Virginia, Kentucky, Ohio

A part of Virginia until 1863, when the west of Virginia deserted the Confederacy and joined the Yankees. A very beautiful state (though not as dramatic as the far West), but wrecked by man in places: ugly little farms and ugly big coal-mines deface the landscape. Rather hillbilly in outlook.

THE ATLANTIC AND CENTRAL EAST-COAST STATES

(Delaware, Maryland, New Jersey, Virginia, North Carolina and Washington DC)

A rather warmer climate than that of New England and the north-east characterises these states, with much milder winters (though sometimes with days or even weeks of snow) and rather warmer summers, again with greater extremes of temperature as you move inland. Rainfall is comparable with New England and the north-west.

Coastal farms are mostly marginal by Midwestern standards, but intensively farmed, especially for market gardening. This whole area is also one of the most industrially important in the US, from primary metal production (especially copper) and coal strip-mining to manufactured goods.

Appendix 1: Compendium

Delaware
State capital Dover
Area 2,000 square miles
Population 600,000
Neighbouring states Pennsylvania, New Jersey, Maryland

Another small state, low-lying, mostly rural, and rather relaxed. Little industry except Du Pont; Delaware is something of a Du Pont fief. Big air-force base. Excellent seafood.

Maryland
State capital Annapolis
Area 10,580 square miles
Population 4,000,000
Neighbouring states Pennsylvania, Delaware, Virginia, West Virginia

An odd-shaped state, which peters out to the west. Baltimore is an important navy base. A mix of agriculture and industry, with the latter predominating: both are very diversified.

New Jersey
State capital Trenton
Area 7,840 square miles
Population 7,500,000
Neighbouring states New York, Delaware, Pennsylvania

Once known as 'The Garden State' for its rich agriculture and beautiful countryside, now chiefly famous for industry and a series of tacky resorts, notably Atlantic City where gambling is legal. Still pleasant in parts, but you have to look hard to find them.

Virginia
State capital Richmond
Area 40,800 square miles
Population 5,500,000
Neighbouring states Maryland, North Carolina, Tennessee, Kentucky, West Virginia

Originally founded as an agricultural domain of Britain, Virginia remains agricultural to this day: cotton, corn and tobacco are the best-known (and most traditional) crops, but others are increasingly important – especially soybeans.

172

North Carolina
State capital Raleigh
Area 52,700 square miles
Population 6,000,000
Neighbouring states Virginia, South Carolina, Georgia, Tennessee.
Long Atlantic coastline.

Agricultural; famous for cotton and tobacco, but now diversified.
The beginning of the real South. Much fishing along the coast –
formerly commercial, now often recreational. A centre of industrial-
isation, especially textiles: the Carolinas contain 70 per cent of the
cotton-spinning spindles in the US.

Washington DC

The District of Columbia houses the nation's capital, so that no
state shall be able to claim the honour – though geographically it
was carved out of Maryland, and Virginia seems to regard it with a
proprietary air. There is no elected local government here. Area 69
square miles; population under 1,000,000 and falling, as government employees move into suburbs in neighbouring states.

THE SOUTHERN ATLANTIC STATES
(South Carolina, Georgia and Florida)

These three states are geographically very diverse. South Carolina
is much like North Carolina, only warmer; Georgia is slightly
warmer again, but with considerable extremes of climate inland;
and Florida is sub-tropical, hot and humid.

Florida
State capital Tallahassee
Area 58,500 square miles
Population 10,000,000
Neighbouring states Georgia, Alabama

Part of the booming Sunbelt and a favoured resort area for the East
Coast. Still unspoiled, not to say downright primitive, in parts:
famous for shortage of law and order.

Georgia
State capital Atlanta
Area 58,870 square miles
Population 5,500,000
Neighbouring states North Carolina, South Carolina, Florida,
Alabama, Tennessee

It took parts of Georgia until World War II to recover from the Civil War: Sherman's destruction of Atlanta set the state back half a century. Still agricultural, but increasingly (at least in the south) a new Sunbelt state. Atlanta is concerned primarily with administration and distribution; industry (including aerospace) is mostly in smaller cities in the state.

South Carolina
State capital Columbia
Area 31,050 square miles
Population 3,000,000
Neighbouring states North Carolina, Georgia. Long Atlantic coastline.

Another agricultural Southern state, but with an increasing tendency to process its own products rather than to export them to other states (see North Carolina also). Tourism of increasing importance, especially along the coast. Much historical interest.

THE SOUTH
(Alabama, Arkansas, Kentucky, Louisiana, Mississippi, Tennessee)

Warm, often humid, summers and cold snowy winters characterise the Southern states. In most (if not all) of these states, racial prejudice is alive and well.

Alabama
State capital Montgomery
Area 51,600 square miles
Population 4,000,000
Neighbouring states Tennessee, Georgia, Florida, Mississippi. Small Gulf of Mexico coastline.

The archetypal cotton state, deprived of most of its coastline by an extension of Florida. Potentially, rather than actually, a Sunbelt state, though NASA's largest facility is located here. Iron and steel around Birmingham. Inland, still primarily agricultural and rather backward.

Arkansas
State capital Little Rock
Area 53,100 square miles
Population 2,000,000
Neighbouring states Tennessee, Mississippi, Louisiana, Texas, Oklahoma, Missouri

Sometimes thought of as a Western state, but more tied to the

South in attitudes and (especially) agriculture: rice and cotton are the main crops, and poultry farming is growing in importance. The Ozarks are the home of real hillbillies – in fact, the whole state is one of 'good ole boys'.

Kentucky
State capital Frankfort
Area 40,400 square miles
Population 3,500,000
Neighbouring states Ohio, West Virginia, Virginia, Tennessee, Missouri, Illinois, Indiana

Famed for horse ranching and tobacco, as well as for coal mining on an enormous scale in the east. In the north, there is also primary metal production and manufacture. Very poor in the Appalachians; readers who have seen the film *The Coal Miner's Daughter* will have a good idea of what they are like.

Louisiana
State capital Baton Rouge
Area 48,500 square miles
Population 4,000,000
Neighbouring states Mississippi, Texas, Arkansas

Traditionally agricultural, and noted for its network of natural waterways: not just the Mississippi River, but also lakes, rivers and *bayous*. Forestry is widespread, especially slash pine for pulp; there is a flourishing paper industry. A great deal of fishing. New Orleans is a major port, and an even greater tourist attraction.

Mississippi
State capital Jackson
Area 47,700 square miles
Population 2,500,000
Neighbouring states Tennessee, Alabama, Louisiana, Arkansas

Agricultural (cotton) again, and often poor in outlying areas: average income in Mississippi is way below the national average, and about *half* that of Alaska. Shipbuilding at Pascagoula; other industry sparse and light.

Tennessee
State capital Nashville
Area 42,250 square miles
Population 4,500,000
Neighbouring states Kentucky, Virginia, North Carolina, Georgia, Alabama, Mississippi, Arkansas, Missouri

Cotton and hardwood lumber are Tennessee's major sources of income, along with prosperous tobacco and dairy farms around Nashville, but out in the hills there are still small farms, poverty, and a 'hillbilly' way of life.

THE CENTRAL UNITED STATES

(Illinois, Iowa, Kansas, Minnesota, Missouri, Nebraska, North Dakota, Oklahoma, South Dakota, Texas, Wisconsin)

These states are a very mixed bag. In terms of rainfall, they exhibit similar summer rainfall to their eastern neighbours, but winter rain (or snow) fall is lower, though only southernmost Texas is really dry. The enormous distance from north to south is reflected in a considerable variation in temperature, with Chicago winters really bitter (though summers are hot and muggy), while Texas is rarely very cold, at least by American standards, and has very warm summers which are, however, tempered by the Gulf of Mexico. In the middle, typical continental weather patterns mean good agricultural growing conditions with extremes of temperature somewhat greater than those of the UK, but without the ultimate extremes of heat and cold found in the south-west and the north-east respectively.

Illinois
State capital Springfield
Area 56,400 square miles
Population 11,500,000
Neighbouring states Indiana, Kentucky, Missouri, Iowa, Wisconsin.Chicago is on Lake Michigan.

A great deal of industry, including steel and oil, especially in the north; Chicago is one of the authors' least favourite cities. Other mines (besides iron) include lead and zinc, but there is plenty of agriculture (including a little-known wine industry), mainly in the south.

Iowa
State capital Des Moines
Area 56,280 square miles
Population 3,000,000
Neighbouring states Wisconsin, Illinois, Missouri, Nebraska, South Dakota, Minnesota

A real Midwestern corn-belt state, also with hogs and cattle. Not much industry, but a lot of administration – finance, insurance, etc – in common with neighbouring corn-belt states.

Kansas
State capital Topeka
Area 82,280 square miles
Population 2,500,000
Neighbouring states Nebraska, Missouri, Oklahoma, Colorado

The 'breadbasket of America', where wheat-fields stretched to the horizon before overproduction led to federal subsidies *not* to grow wheat. Now more diversified, with maize, sorghum and soy. Some cattle farming (with first-class beef), but better known for being the route through which Texas cattle were driven in the 1870s and 1880s, to be 'finished' on corn before slaughter. Trades on its (highly idealised and reconstructed) cowboy past, but the Bible-belt present is altogether more obvious.

Minnesota
State capital St Paul
Area 84,000 square miles
Population 4,000,000
Neighbouring states Wisconsin, Iowa, South Dakota, North Dakota (also borders Canada)

Spectacular scenery in the still largely unspoiled north, towards the Canadian border. Iron strip-mining on an awesome scale; wood-pulp lumber is the other major industry. Farming is mostly hay and dairy.

Missouri
State capital Jefferson City
Area 69,670 square miles
Population 5,000,000
Neighbouring states Illinois, Kentucky, Tennessee, Arkansas, Oklahoma, Kansas, Nebraska, Iowa

The beginning of the Midwest, with all that it implies: wide open spaces, the Bible-belt, and agriculture. Rather more interesting scenery than its western neighbours, with the Lake of the Ozarks apparently very attractive.

Nebraska
State capital Lincoln
Area 77,250 square miles
Population 1,500,000
Neighbouring states South Dakota, Iowa, Kansas, Colorado, Wyoming

Known as the Great Plains State, Nebraska is bordered by South Dakota, Iowa, Kansas, Colorado and Wyoming. Mostly extremely flat and given over to agriculture and (especially) stock-raising.

177

North Dakota
State capital Bismarck
Area 70,660 square miles
Population 700,000
Neighbouring states Minnesota, South Dakota, Montana (also borders Canada)

The rich Midwestern agricultural soil peters out in the wheat-growing Dakotas, until cattle-raising is the only practical kind of farming – and even then, markets are not readily to hand. Little industry and a sparse population. Oil and lignite are exploited in the south of the state.

Oklahoma
State capital Oklahoma City
Area 69,920 square miles
Population 3,000,000
Neighbouring states Kansas, Missouri, Arkansas, Texas, New Mexico,Colorado

Wheat and beef, with an increasing reliance on petroleum. Very Bible-belt, but likes to play on its 'Wild West' past, which is now heavily idealised and romanticised – and sanitised.

South Dakota
State capital Pierre
Area 77,050 square miles
Population 700,000
Neighbouring states North Dakota, Minnesota, Iowa, Nebraska, Wyoming, Montana

'The challenge state', with a temperature range of 150°F (85°C) from summer to winter (though you would have to pick your locations). A sparsely populated prairie state, with some oil and lignite to the north; the country's major gold-producing area.

Texas
State capital Austin
Area 267,340 square miles
Population 14,000,000
Neighbouring states Oklahoma, Arkansas, Louisiana, New Mexico (also borders Mexico). (Coastline in Gulf of Mexico)

Over a quarter of a million square miles of Texans; a fearsome thought. Cattle barons were the first plutocrats, followed by oil barons, though cotton and lumber also made fortunes. A 'sunrise' state, with heavy NASA investment and much high-tech industry. The Western pattern of large air-force and other military bases begins to be seen in the less populated areas of Texas. Houston is a major port.

Wisconsin
State capital Madison
Area 56,150 square miles
Population 5,000,000
Neighbouring states Michigan, Illinois, Iowa, Minnesota. A Great Lakes state

'America's Dairyland', but also plenty of industry, heavy and light. Milwaukee is famous for beer and Harley-Davidson. Much attractive scenery.

THE WEST AND FAR WEST
(Arizona, California, Colorado, Idaho, Montana, Nevada,
New Mexico, Oregon, Utah, Washington, Wyoming)

Some people say they can breathe more easily in the 'big sky' country of the Midwest, but the authors prefer to breathe the air of freedom in the Far West, where the scenery is stunning, the Bible-belt has mostly petered out, and each state guards not only its own freedom, but also that of its citizens – though California is increasingly regulated, perhaps due to the endless migration of Easterners many of whom have socialist tendencies. Native Californians prefer to be left alone, hence the bumper sticker 'IF YOU ♥ NEW YORK – GO THERE'.

The south-west is mostly either desert or (inland) high plains cattle country, though the California coast is very fertile and is a major agricultural exporter. In the north-west, there is less desert, and more stock-raising and agriculture. The four states of Utah, Colorado, New Mexico and Arizona meet at 'four corners', the only place in the US where this happens; this is why some of the 'neighbouring states' information below is qualified with 'just!'.

Arizona
State capital Phoenix
Area 113,500 square miles
Population 3,000,000
Neighbouring states Utah (just!), New Mexico, California (also borders Mexico)

A very diverse state, with a mixture of agriculture and desert, mountains and plains, and of course the Grand Canyon. A favoured state for Sunbelt relocation, though with a slight Bible-belt tinge which can become obtrusive.

Appendix 1: Compendium

California
State capital Sacramento
Area 158,700 square miles
Population 23,000,000
Neighbouring states Oregon, Nevada, Arizona (also borders Mexico)

A surprisingly long state – almost 1,000 miles – along the Pacific coast. Something for everyone, though some find LA seasonless and characterless; others love it. The Sunbelt state par excellence, but with a surprisingly rural north, beyond Sacramento, where there is also considerably more climatic variation. Contains some of the most beautiful places in the world, and is easily the most popular state with British immigrants and visitors.

Colorado
State capital Denver
Area 104,250 square miles
Population 3,000,000
Neighbouring states Wyoming, Nebraska, Kansas, Oklahoma, New Mexico, Arizona (just!), Utah

Traditionally a cowboy and 'wild-west' state, now much wider-based with mining, industry (especially Sunbelt relocation and aerospace), and finance, banking, etc, for which Denver is a major regional centre whose importance stretches well outside Colorado.

Idaho
State capital Boise
Area 83,550 square miles
Population 900,000
Neighbouring states Montana, Wyoming, Utah, Nevada, Oregon, Washington (also borders Canada)

Mining in the mountains, and agriculture and stock-raising wherever the land is flat enough. Famous for potatoes. Much very beautiful scenery, especially in the north and to the east.

Montana
State capital Helena
Area 147,140 square miles
Population 800,000
Neighbouring states North Dakota, South Dakota, Wyoming, Idaho (also borders Canada)

Wonderful scenery, including Yellowstone and Glacier National Parks. Montana was the scene of a gold rush in 1864, and silver was discovered shortly afterwards, but copper mining has provided more wealth than either. Industries are mixed. Montana also has plenty of agriculture, and is noted for high-quality beef and dairy cattle.

Nevada
State capital Carson City
Area 110,540 square miles
Population 800,000
Neighbouring states Idaho, Utah, California, Oregon

Mostly desert; some mining, mostly abandoned; only two major cities (Las Vegas and Reno), both of which make most of their living from gambling. Prostitution is legal (though not licensed in towns of more than 200,000 people), and there is a general and exhilarating air of independence from Eastern prudery and too-affluent Californian neo-socialism. Large military bases, including nuclear-weapons testing.

New Mexico
State capital Santa Fe NM
Area 121,660 square miles
Population 1,000,000
Neighbouring states Colorado, Oklahoma, Texas, Arizona, Utah (just!) (also borders Mexico)

Mountains, high plains, some desert, and the typical Western military establishments, such as White Sands Missile Test Range. Traditionally cattle country, a 'wild west' state, and very much Spanish America in its architecture. Taos is a famous artists' and writers' community; other towns also remain firmly rooted in the past. Much Native American culture, and several reservations. Stunning scenery in many places.

Oregon
State capital Salem
Area 96,900 square miles
Population 2,500,000
Neighbouring states Washington, Idaho, Nevada, California

Beautiful coastline, rugged country, agriculture (especially fruit). Thinly populated, because although potentially prosperous in *absolute* terms, in *relative* terms it is overshadowed by California – where the weather is better too!

Utah

State capital Salt Lake City
Area 84,900 square miles
Population 1,500,000
Neighbouring states Wyoming, Colorado, New Mexico (just!), Arizona, Nevada, Idaho

The Mormon state, from which the Latterday Saints have managed to fashion a (reasonably) productive agricultural area in what is mostly unpromising, but often staggeringly beautiful, desert. Some mining, including the world's largest copper pit, but increasingly reliant on tourism – and well worth visiting. *Not* oppressively religious, though the Mormons will gently try to convert you.

Washington

State capital Olympia
Area 68,200 square miles
Population 4,000,000
Neighbouring states Idaho, Oregon (also borders Canada)

Seattle was formerly the busiest port on the west Coast, especially for lumber export. Now the state is very rural and pleasantly relaxed, though there is some aerospace industry. Soft fruit farming (including wine grapes) inland.

Wyoming

State capital Cheyenne
Area 98,000 square miles
Population 500,000
Neighbouring states Montana, South Dakota, Nebraska, Colorado, Utah, Idaho

The 'cowboy state', consisting mainly of high grasslands (4,000–7,000ft/1,000–2,000m). Straddles the Continental Divide. Much stunning scenery, including parts of Yellowstone National Park and Grand Teton National Park.

ALASKA AND HAWAII

As usual, these two states do not fall into any convenient category, and are considered separately.

Alaska

State capital Juneau
Area 586,400 square miles
Population 500,000

The 'Last Frontier'. Very rugged, with great extremes of temperature; only approachable as a vacation land in summer. The main industries are various forms of mineral exploitation.

Hawaii
State capital Honolulu
Area 6,430 square miles
Population 1,000,000

Vacation country, military bases, pineapple and other tropical produce (especially macadamia nuts), and surprisingly unspoiled away from the touristy bits. Hawaii is the biggest in a chain of islands which also includes Maui, Kahoolawe, Lanai, Molokai, Oahu (where Honolulu is), Kauai, and Niihau.

Appendix 2
Useful Addresses

Telephone numbers for the organisations below are not given since calls rarely elicit a useful response. A brief letter, on the other hand will usually prompt a form-letter reply, with a much more useful local address and telephone number.

American Automobile Association (AAA)
8111 Gatehouse Road
Falls Church VA 22047
(The largest automobile association in the US: provides insurance, travel and other services including International Driving Permits.)

British Embassy
3100 Massachusetts Avenue NW
Washington DC 20008
(There are also Consular Offices in other cities.)

Chamber of Commerce, National Office
1615 H Street NW
Washington DC 20062

Greyhound Lines Inc
Greyhound Tower
Phoenix AZ 85077
(The largest bus company in the US.)

Housing and Urban Development Department
451 7th Street SW
Washington DC 20410
(A source for useful publications such as *Buying a Home: Don't Forget the Closing Costs, Buying Lots from Developers, Before Buying Land, Mobile Home Park Financing* and *Real Estate Settlement Procedure.*)

Immigration and Naturalization Service
425 Eye Street NW
Washington DC 20536
(This address will be useful only to request very general information on the addresses of regional offices.)

Appendix 2: Useful Addresses

Internal Revenue Service
111 Constitution Avenue NW
Washington DC 20224
(As above, this address would only be useful to find out the address
to write to for other information. For forms distribution alone there
are eleven regional centres.)

National Association of Real Estate Brokers
1101 14th Street NW
Washington DC 20005

National Association of Realtors
777 14th Street NW
Washington DC 20005

National Automobile Club
One Market Plaza
San Francisco CA 94105

National Education Association
1201 16th Street NW
Washington DC 20036
(The best source for information on teaching in the US.)

National Home Buyers and Home Owners Association
1528 18th Street NW
Washington DC 20036
(This is an advocacy group to promote consumer interests in
housing. They publish the *Homebuyers Checklist*.)

National Insurance Consumer Organization
344 Commerce Street
Alexandria VA 22314
(This organization will provide information to consumers buying
insurance.)

National Railroad Passenger Corporation (Amtrak)
400 North Capitol Street NW
Washington DC 20001

Social Security Administration
6401 Security Boulevard
Baltimore MD 21235
(Most contact with the Social Security would take place at the
regional office and in person.)

Trailways Inc (Buses)
1500 Jackson Street
Dallas TX 75201

US Customs Service
1301 Constitution Avenue NW
Washington DC 20229
(There are also regional offices in Boston, New York, Miami, New Orleans, Houston, Los Angeles and Chicago. Most questions which you will have prior to leaving can be answered by the customs desk at the US Embassy.)

US Embassy (All Departments)
24 Grosvenor Square
London W1
(Services are available including a Commerce Library, information on taxes, immigration and customs. Any booklets may be requested from the appropriate department.)

Bibliography

There are innumerable guide books to the United States, and we suggest that you browse at your local bookstore: which ones appeal to you will depend on your own taste, income and interests. Alternatively, the US Embassy in Grosvenor Square maintains an excellent library which is open to the public on weekdays from 10am to 5pm; ask for the Commerce Library. What follows is a personal and very limited selection of books which we have found useful.

Once you are in the United States, the most useful single book is probably your local telephone directory.

Classified Directory, Classified Directory Publishers Ltd, Niagara Falls, New York 14302
(Similar to a Yellow Pages, as well as advertising the index reads as follows: Weights and Measures, Financial, Government, Sports, Calendars, Embassies and Consulates, Ski Resorts, US Facts, World, Religion, Business and Government, Science and Nature, Immigration and Naturalization, Health, and Statistics.)

Encyclopedia of Associations, Vol. I part 1 and 2, Denise S. Akey (Ed), Gale Research Co, Book Tower, Detroit, MI 48226
(A great source for finding special-interest groups. Includes bicycling, darts, soccer, rugby, left-handed golf, and cricket – but beware because they also list the cricket *growers'* association.)

Fodor's America, Hodder and Stoughton, London, Sydney and Auckland
(Probably the best general guide, but so much aimed at the affluent middle-class 'middle America' that it puts some people off. Revised annually.)

Frommer's assorted *Guides*, Arthur Frommer Inc, New York
(Frommer was the man who thought of the 'Europe on $5 a Day' idea, and has (deservedly) done very well out of it; his organisation offers several guides to different parts of the United States. They do show you how to do it on the cheap, but they are not always as up-to-date as they should be, and the prose style is often gushing to the point of being nauseating. Revised annually.)

Bibliography

Information Please Almanac, Houghton Mifflin Co, Boston, MA
(A very useful book for anyone interested in the US. It includes the text of the Constitution and its amendments, information on taxes, history, the military, sports, arts and useful addresses such as the state and city tourism offices. It is an excellent overview and reference book. Revised annually.)

Thomas Register Inbound Traffic Guide, Vol. 19, Thomas Publishing Co, One Penn Plaza, New York, NY 10117
(This is probably most useful to the business person. It is an annual transportation-services directory listing air express, airlines, barges, customs, export services, freight services, ports, public warehouses, railroads, shippers' associations, steamships, transportation brokers and trucking. Revised annually.)

USA West, Lonely Planet Publications, South Yarra, Victoria, Australia
(A lively and interesting guide to the West on the cheap, but too much oriented towards ageing (or neo-) hippies for many people's taste. The places they rate as 'expensive' are usually excellent value and well within most people's budgets.)

Washington Information Directory, Congressional Quarterly Inc, 1414 22nd Street NW, Washington DC 20037
(A complete guide to governmental departments and agencies, as well as Washington-based consumer advocacy groups.)

Acknowledgements

A book such as this must depend on help and information from many sources. While it is impossible to acknowledge all of those who contributed ideas and factual content, the authors would like to extend their particular thanks to the following:

First and foremost, to Frances's parents, Arthur and Marion Schultz, whose warm and generous hospitality permitted us to stay for much longer in the United States than would otherwise have been possible while doing the final research for this book. The same thanks are due to Drs Boyd and Lucille Collins, without whose kindness we should not have spent anything like so long in Los Angeles. Mr and Mrs F. Fisher Jr, of Boston, were also extremely kind, as was their younger son Hamilton and his wife Anya. Still on the East Coast, Mr and Mrs C. Truscott have always been kind hosts in Dover, Delaware, and moving inland we are indebted to Mr and Mrs D. Schultz for their hospitality in Ashland, Kentucky. Back in California, Herb Agid has long been a warm friend, and we particularly appreciate the time spent with him in his cabin in the Gold Country; and without M and Mme J.-M. Lofficier, this book would probably never have been written. Mr and Mrs D. Collins and Mr and Mrs K. Schultz furnished many valuable insights into American business life, as well as being fun to be with.

The Internal Revenue Service in Los Angeles, and the Social Security, Customs and Immigration offices in Long Beach, California, were very helpful, as were the customs offices in Avonmouth, near Bristol, England, and of course the American Embassy in London. For information on insurance, as well as for help in arranging insurance on many trips, we must thank Downend Insurance of Downend, Bristol, and for information on quarantine, we are indebted to Meg Purnell-Carpenter of Overhill Kennels in Whitchurch, near Bristol.

Finally, we would like to express our most sincere thanks to Mr and Mrs H. Salmon, an American–British couple like ourselves, who read through the manuscript and made many valuable suggestions – although, of course, any mistakes remain our own.

R.W.H. and F.E.S.
California and Bristol, England

Index

Index